**Praise for**

I've never read a book like this before. I mean, even this question, "Are we willing to sometimes be the weak ones?" made me think deeply. Kevan and Tommy have done us a favor here. I've never thought about hospitality this way. So good!

**Brant Hansen**
Radio/podcast host and bestselling author of *Unoffendable* and *The Men We Need*

I have long believed that it's hard to produce good gifts—in stories, art, or almost any endeavor—apart from pain. Birth pains bring longed-for life, and a cross comes before a crown. Kevan's life is a story of changing pain into powerful gifts, turning limits into launchpads. In this new book, Kevan brings more hard-fought truth to us, alongside his friend Tommy. Between Kevan's disability and Tommy's work as a pastor, they together have lessons for us from the front. And, surprise, these lessons are all about the power of weakness in this wonderful, worthwhile book.

**S. D. Smith**
Author of The Green Ember series and *The Found Boys*

Kevan and Tommy have written a simple yet profound book that delves into the most fundamental of human needs, the need to belong. Their work moved me so much, I wish I would have written something similar years ago—much like Kevan, I have a disability and God has organically created a wonderful community of friends that have gathered around my "need." The result is true "community" in which we all feel secure, have purpose, receive reward, and are free to offer our authentic selves to one another. However, Kevan Chandler and Tommy Shelton take this idea much further in *The Hospitality of Need*. Their stories and insights provide a powerful response to people's desperate longing to feel accepted, valued, and supported. And this remarkable book does not stop there. It goes further to describe how the reader can create a fulfilling community that brings health and wholeness to everyone. Honestly, *The Hospitality of Need* shows the way God created us to be. The book you hold in your hands gets five stars from me!

**Joni Eareckson Tada**
Founder of the Joni and Friends International Disability Center

# THE HOSPITALITY
# OF NEED

MOODY PUBLISHERS

CHICAGO

Edited by Ashleigh Slater
Interior design: Puckett Smartt
Cover design: Faceout Studio, Molly von Borstel
Cover illustration of Christ and the Samaritan Woman by Alessandro Moretto copyright © 2024 ZU_09/iStock (660458502). All rights reserved.
Author photo: Luke Thompson

ISBN: 978-0-8024-3608-5

Originally delivered by fleets of horse-drawn wagons, the affordable paperbacks from D. L. Moody's publishing house resourced the church and served everyday people. Now, after more than 125 years of publishing and ministry, Moody Publishers' mission remains the same—even if our delivery systems have changed a bit. For more information on other books (and resources) created from a biblical perspective, go to www.moodypublishers.com or write to:

Moody Publishers
820 N. LaSalle Boulevard
Chicago, IL 60610

1 3 5 7 9 10 8 6 4 2

*Printed in the United States of America*

*This book is dedicated to our friends.*

# Contents

# An Introduction
# to the Idea

ome time back, I had the privilege of cohosting a conference session with Kevan Chandler, rooted in many of the same ideas enumerated in this book. While my thoughts on the topic were in some ways more abstract, Kevan's were the powerful and hard-won wisdom of lived experience, bearing witness to how his own yielded needs have been built by God into a life-giving hub of hospitality. My primary contribution to our session was simply to relate one particular story and then get out of the way. At Kevan's invitation, I'm happy to repeat that same story here in hopes that it might, in some way, set the table for the rich feast of the chapters to follow.

During the idealistic span of my late twenties and early thirties, I spent an extended season fixated on the idea of *community*. After impulse-buying a log home on acreage in West Tennessee—a move that geographically isolated us for a year-and-a-half—my wife and I moved back to town and neighborhood with a hunger for those aspects of life-giving relationships whose loss we'd felt so acutely. For starters, we chose a neighborhood based on its proximity to our church.

We were newly committed to the idea of making intentional choices that would counteract the natural tendency toward isolation, which might result in the cultivation and flourishing of a vital Christian community. We were on something of a mission.

Almost immediately, we joined a church home group. The weekly gathering was hosted and led by a psychologist who held a position at a major university. I was delighted to discover that he, too, was fixated on the idea of building and fostering Christian community. It seemed we'd found a like-minded fellowship where our young family might explore and implement those aspirations.

For the next two years, that small group gathered on a weekly basis. Discussions focused heavily on topics of community. *How do we intentionally create it?* Amidst grill-outs and get-togethers, we sifted such questions and tried to pursue whatever we thought might foster the sort of community we so longed for.

But somehow, we never quite got there.

At the end of two years, there was a particular Sunday evening when we gathered as usual—but the meeting took an abrupt and unexpected turn. After a few minutes of greetings and pleasantries, our group leader announced, "My wife and I have been talking, and we've decided to disband this group. We've reached the conclusion that amidst the busyness and demands of our present-day culture, community just isn't possible."

That was it.

They were shutting down the experiment. After two years focused on trying to find ways to build community, and after evaluation and consideration of what we had or hadn't managed to do, that was their verdict: *Go live your own lives. In today's world—at least in our Western culture—community isn't a realistic goal, even amongst followers of Jesus.*

For most of the group, it was a sucker punch.

We disbanded, scratching our heads, wondering if there had been any point to our efforts.

Not long after, I took my family to visit my grandmother in the Midwest. She was eager to take us one afternoon to meet a family from her church. As an introvert, I wasn't particularly enthused by the prospect, but because it was so clearly important to my grandmother, I agreed to go. In short order, we were driving to this family's house a little way outside of town.

It's been more than two decades since. Some of the details are lost to me. Did the family have four kids or five kids? I can't remember. What I do remember is that as we drove there, my grandma told us that the family had twins, a boy and a girl. When they were toddlers, the boy had wandered out to the patio area without anyone noticing. A few minutes later, when they realized he was missing and mounted a frantic search, they discovered him facedown in the swimming pool.

Now, it was a few years later. The boy had survived, but his brain had been deprived of oxygen long enough that severe, permanent damage had occurred. He couldn't speak, walk, or crawl. He couldn't do anything for himself. He now required constant care.

At this point, the socially awkward part of my self—which admittedly is *most* of my self—was bracing for the inevitable painfulness of the ensuing interactions. I remembered the extreme awkwardness I sometimes felt as a child when my mom would take me along to visit a stroke victim named J.J., who couldn't speak. J.J. was aware of his surroundings but could only laugh or cry as a means of expressing his thoughts and feelings. He would suddenly burst into sobs when he saw me. I think it was just his way of expressing gratitude that we'd come to visit. But as a kid, I didn't know what to do with that unsettling gush of emotion. I had no natural instinct to guide me toward a fitting response. I feared this visit with my grandmother's friends might feel similar.

My trepidations, as it turned out, were utterly misplaced.

We were greeted cheerfully at the door by the boy's mom. She was genuinely joyful and utterly unpretentious. She took us into the front room, where the little boy lay on a hospital-type bed. She introduced him to us and us to him. I think he might have slowly smiled, which was probably the limit of his ability to interact. There was a woman sitting on a chair beside the boy's bed. We were introduced to her and learned the story of her connection to the family.

Years earlier, shortly after the accident, this woman had heard of their plight during a prayer request time at church. She had never met the family that had suffered the tragedy, but she said God nonetheless impressed on her that she was to sit for an hour every day with the little boy and pray for him. So, for multiple years, that's what she had been doing: sitting with the boy, talking to him, praying for him, and also giving the parents a daily break from the routine of care. As a result, she had become joined to this family. Their lives were now deeply and meaningfully intertwined.

From there, we moved to the dining room table, where our hosts offered snacks and drinks. We sat awhile in conversation, getting to know the parents and some of the kids. There was no formality to any of it, but their hospitality was easy, generous, unforced, and welcoming. I found myself at ease, drawn out of my own protective shell.

We were soon interrupted by a middle-aged man who walked in from the garage without bothering to knock. He was slightly abashed at first, suddenly finding himself amongst people he didn't know. His mannerisms suggested someone at least as socially awkward as myself. But our hostess insisted he come sit down at the table, and people shifted their seats to make room for him. So he joined us, and we were introduced. He was there performing maintenance on something.

They recounted the story of how the doctors had told them their son might benefit from oxygen therapy, as it could accelerate the natural, reparative work of the brain. But no hyperbaric oxygen chamber was available for treatments within a two- or three-hour drive from where they lived. So, it simply wasn't feasible to transport their son several times a week for oxygen therapy.

When this gentleman, who also attended their church, learned of that dilemma, he took it upon himself to research what was involved in constructing hyperbaric oxygen chambers. He drew up what he believed was a feasible plan and presented it to them. They gave the go-ahead, and he proceeded to build a fully functioning hyperbaric oxygen chamber in their garage at a small fraction of the prohibitive cost of a typical chamber. As a natural result of his time spent at their house addressing that need, he too had been grafted into their family—and now held a standing privilege to walk into their home without knocking.

Not long after the chamber was built, the family became aware—through their doctors—that it wasn't just their son who needed oxygen therapy. There were scores of folks in their region who might benefit from ongoing access to such treatments. So, they freely opened their home and the use of their oxygen chamber to others with medical needs. Now, a steady stream of doctor-referred patients came to their house for therapy. It was an act of open generosity, a service rendered in the name of Jesus. And through their warm and welcoming hospitality, they naturally got to know those people who now visited their house on a regular basis, building friendships and praying for and ministering to others in need or crisis.

There were other folks involved with the family as well. Their house seemed a beehive of people, laughing, serving, praying, fellowshipping. My grandmother, now a widow, would go over once a week to serve in whatever ways she might.

I sat quietly for awhile, observing all of this, and thought, here's this little boy who can do nothing for himself. His story is one that involves profound loss, weakness, and inability. And yet, in this place of tragedy, there was also real joy. There was a deep sense of peace.

All these people, their lives now vitally intertwined, were here because they had moved—in ways big or small—toward this heartbreaking need. Confronted with the suffering of this boy and this family, rather than passing by on the other side of the road,[1] these were people who had said *yes* and responded in practical and meaningful ways.

And in so doing—even though it was not their agenda or even on their radar—the result was that a vital Christian community had organically formed.

And at the hub of it all was this helpless little boy.

That day, I watched the people coming and going. I observed the love and care they all had, not just for the boy, but for one another, and I had an epiphany I've never fully recovered from:

> *This is the answer I've been looking for in a place I never thought to look.*
> *This is how Christian community forms.*
> *It forms around weakness.*
> *It forms around need.*
> *Christian community is the natural—perhaps even inevitable— outgrowth of bearing one another's burdens and so fulfilling the law of Christ.*

It turns out you can't analyze community into existence. You can't will it or talk it into being. You can't create authentic Christian community by focusing on yourself or your group and what you want to build. That's not how it works. That's where, in our home group, we'd gotten it wrong.

---

1. Luke 10:30–37.

Community is what happens when we move toward need, toward weakness, toward brokenness, or when we allow others to move toward our need, our weakness, and our brokenness. Weakness and need become a sort of grace reactor fueling the formation of real community. It happens as followers of Jesus respond in compassion, kindness, mercy, and love. Because when we move toward the meeting of needs, we are also moving inevitably toward one another—which is perhaps to say, we are all in that merciful movement actually moving toward Jesus in whom we are joined and held together as one body.

The needs we move toward might be physical, practical, and obvious, as they were at that house. Or they might be the less visible emotional or spiritual needs that mark each of us. And it might just be our willingness to open our own weaknesses to those who are walking with us and bear their burdens in turn, which ultimately serves as the catalyst for community.

This leads us to very important questions—ones that sit at the heart of what Kevan and Tommy have to offer the rest of us in the pages of this book: *Are we willing to sometimes be the weak ones? Are we willing to sometimes be the ones who are broken, helpless, or in need? Will we allow community to be built around our own weaknesses and needs? Will we offer—not just our strengths and our assets—but even our weaknesses and our needs to God, asking that He use those very things for the building of His kingdom?*

I'm convinced that the building of Christian community is the work of God from beginning to end. I now think all it requires of us is that we keep showing up, that we faithfully respond to the needs of others who are also showing up, and finally, that we are willing to let our own needs be exposed in front of those trusted fellow pilgrims with whom we share this journey. After all, if I can't learn to let go of my own pretense, my self-protective instincts, and my desire to be perceived as a strong, independent, and autonomous person who "has it all together," how could I ever foster any real relationship with another person? If what I'm offering is, in the end, only a curated mask or a slick veneer, what hope for real, life-giving connection is there?

Paul tells us in 1 Corinthians 1:26–29,

> Brothers and sisters, think of what you were when you were called. Not many of you were wise by human standards; not many were influential; not many were of noble birth. But God chose the foolish things of the world to shame the wise; God chose the weak things of the world to shame the strong. God chose the lowly things of this world and the despised things—and the things that are not—to nullify the things that are, so that no one may boast before him.[2]

God delights in choosing and using as vessels for His glory those who are poor in spirit, those of us who know that we're weak, who know that we could never accomplish in our own strength the good works to which we are called. And it is His good pleasure, I'm convinced, to build that kind of people into community and to place them in families.

Christ's body, in its purest expression, is a fellowship of the broken who share this pilgrim journey toward restoration, the eternal kingdom, and the redemption of all things. And that shared movement toward the weaknesses and needs among us and in the world around us is also a movement toward the hospitable heart of Christ, for it is in the heart of our own exposed weakness where we might find the surprising power of Christ most vigorously at work.

Douglas McKelvey
Author of *Every Moment Holy*

---

2. 1 Cor. 1:26–29 NIV.

# Through the Roof

*from Kevan*

There was once a man who was lowered through a roof. He was disabled. We don't know the specifics, what disease he had, or the accident that crippled him. We do know he couldn't walk; his body didn't work right. I relate a lot to this guy, whom the gospel writers simply call "the paralytic."[1] I can't walk; my body doesn't work right. If I had been around in his time, I would have lived out my life lying on a mat like he did.

But that's not the only way I relate to him. He also had friends, like I have. It was his friends who carried him on his mat across town to meet Jesus. And when they got to the packed-out house, they pulled him up onto the roof. They tore open a hole and lowered him into the middle of the room, plopped him right down in front of Jesus. I have friends like this. Good friends who bring me to the feet of Jesus time and time again with every action they take to care for me and to make my life not just possible but abundant. My friends cut holes in roofs every day—in word, deed, laughter, and song—and together, we get to experience Jesus.

Tommy is one such friend. We grew up together in North Carolina,

---

1. Matt. 9:2–8; Mark 2:3–12.

although our deeper friendship began some years later. We reconnected through a mutual friend after Tommy had become a pastor in Tampa, Florida. I have often enjoyed listening to his sermons online, appreciating his reverence for Scripture and his joy in declaring truth. But I have also loved visiting him because I get to see firsthand how he lives throughout his week what he preaches on Sunday morning.

He cares for the vulnerable, celebrates the unseen, and listens to the forgotten. He delights in his wife, cherishes his kids, and honors his parents. And when I come around, he cuts holes in roofs for me. Tommy gladly helps me with the restroom when it's really most inconvenient for him, jumps in to give me a shower without any heads-up, and has welcomed me into his home amid busy family schedules more often than I can say. We have sat together in hard times, rejoiced in fun times, and copiloted a twelve-hour road trip without ever running out of things to talk about.

This is a book about friendship, the kind that God has called us to live in; friendship that goes deep and flourishes, not in spite of our needs but actually through them. In the following pages, you will find my own testimony of how needs (mine and those of others) have ushered my friends and me into deeper fellowship with God and one another. This is paired with Tommy's biblical exposition—primarily from the Gospels-accounted life of Jesus—to scaffold what we believe to be a sound, orthodox concept. While Tommy and I did contribute to each other's chapters, you will notice a name under each title to denote the primary writer so that you know who's being referred to in the first person when applicable.

I have had the amazing honor of pragmatically exploring this idea throughout my life with Tommy and the other men and women who show up in this book. You will read about times when we've done it right on purpose, other times when we've done it right by accident, and times when we haven't done it right at all. We have stepped into each other's needs together, with all its countercultural pace and mess. Cutting holes in roofs ain't pretty! And I struggle with whether that makes me a burden. I'm sure it crossed the paralytic's mind, too, as his friends grunted with every heave-ho up and down. But these friends lower me down as they did him, and I hope that in some way through the process, I'm lowering them down too. As they carry me, help me, and meet my needs, their needs are also met. As they bring me to Jesus, they get closer to Him as well. We have found that while doing things this way may have challenges the world would prefer to avoid, it's a doorway that can lead to healing, growth, and restoration. It leads us together to the feet of Jesus.

There's one more way I relate to the man lowered through the roof. Jesus told him his sins were forgiven, and He's told me the same. But here is where we are different. After forgiving him of his sins, Jesus turned away from the paralytic to address the Pharisees who were there. They were murmuring about Him thinking He could forgive sins, so Jesus called them on it. He asked them which of the two options was easier to say:

1. Your sins are forgiven, or . . .
2. Take up your mat and walk.

"But that you may know that the Son of Man has authority on earth to forgive sins,"[2] and with that, Jesus turned back to the man and told him to get up. And he did! He hopped up, grabbed his mat, and probably danced his way through the crowd to meet his friends outside. Or did he climb back up the ropes to join them on the roof?

---

2. Mark 2:10.

I don't know, but I am guessing it was quite a sight to see for everyone in the room.

I am a paralytic. I have been lowered through roofs to the feet of Jesus. I am lowered every day. And when I was six years old, the King of Kings knelt by my mat, looked me in the eye, and forgave me of my sins. I am forgiven.

But I'm still lying on the mat. What was for the man perhaps thirty seconds—lying there, waiting, between forgiveness and physical healing—has been for me more than thirty years, and it will likely be longer. Maybe a lifetime. Jesus is currently addressing the Pharisees in the room, and I'm waiting—mostly patiently.

I wonder if the man looked up through the hole to his friends in that moment of waiting. I wonder if he winked at them or if they gave him an encouraging thumbs-up. Maybe he kept his eyes on Jesus the whole time, and maybe they did too. That's probably more like it. Whatever the case, he wasn't alone in the waiting, even thirty seconds of it. And I'm not alone either. I guess that's another way I can relate to him. My friends lower me through the roof to the feet of Jesus. He forgives my sins and their sins, too, and they wait with me—I wait with them—for Jesus to faithfully complete the good work He has started in us.

# CHAPTER ONE

# My Family Room

### *from Kevan*

J ust when you think Carolina clay can't get any more orange, the sun begins to set. A wonderful phenomenon happens in those southern hills at dusk. As soon as the sinking sun meets the earth, streaks of fire race across the surface of the world. Houses and trees, neighbors grilling out and kids playing soccer, all the way down to grass blades and rabbits, everything is run through by those final beams of warm light at the end of each day. The blue sky fades into reds and yellows, its aviation-plowed clouds blushing subtle pinks. People glow like embers as they play fetch with their golden dogs on auburn mountainsides. And the hard, orange dirt bakes into tones deeper and richer than a heart can barely handle.

The sunset struck me and my dad in my parents' backyard as we sat on the edge of what you might have thought was a swimming pool, or at least a swimming pool in the making. My dad had just finished digging the foundation for a new room off the back of our house. An airplane mechanic, he had strong hands and creases at the corners of his eyes from seeing things no one else could. He sat with me on the western corner of his work, our backs to the sun. A neighbor came by to see the progress, and they chatted while I played.

I barreled my matchbox cars mercilessly along the burnt orange foundation, a canyon's rim to my six-year-old imagination. One false move and either Batman or the A-Team would plummet to their doom. They dared the fateful ledge at a hundred miles an hour, at least two wheels hanging off at any given time, of course.

Within a few weeks, framing went up, and the concrete was poured. Soon, we had a sealed room, and just in time too. The year was 1992, and my sister's surprise birthday party was Beauty and the Beast themed. People arrived and snuck through the house to hide in the new space. Pink insulation hung between exposed studs, and the floor was still just concrete. But Mom had decorated, and it was a room full of friends. By the look on Connie's face when she rolled in, it might as well have been Disney World itself.

We called it our "family room," and that's just what it was. A place for our family to be together. It's where I first met Aslan as my sister read to me The Chronicles of Narnia. It's where my brother got me hooked on cartoons like *Pinky and the Brain* and *Earth Worm Jim*. My mom introduced me to Winnie-the-Pooh while we curled up on the couch together in that room. My dad taught me how you always start puzzles at the border. And nearly every Christmas morning memory lands me back there.

I also remember laying on the couch in pain after falling out of my wheelchair in the backyard. A few years later, while recovering from a broken right shoulder, I sat in front of paused cartoons on the TV, trying to teach myself how to draw them now with my left hand. In that room is where I first heard bands like Switchfoot and The O.C. Supertones in middle school. And in high school, when my youth pastor gave me an album called *Carried Along*, which spoke to my soul like no music ever had before, guess where I first sat and listened to it?

But the family room was for more than just me and my siblings.

The space—and idea—was much bigger than that. In high school, I hung out with a pretty rowdy crowd, but at my parents' house, many of them tended to fall asleep on the couches. It was the only place they had in their lives where they felt safe enough to let down their guard and rest.

My dad's coworkers and friends also found sanctuary there. He had a commute on third shift, so one morning every week, his vanpool buddies came over for breakfast and Bible study. It was my fourth-grade year when I was homeschooled due to some major surgeries, and I loved those mornings, waking up to a company of giants. I can still hear their roars of laughter and smell the motor oil as a dozen sleep-deprived airplane mechanics filled our family room to study God's Word.

It was our default room for Thanksgiving meals when we (usually me) invited more people than could fit in the dining room. My mom had an old hutch that sat unassumingly against one wall. Behind its old bifold doors, a table was found that could extend across the span of the room, almost all the way to the fireplace. We pushed back the couches countless times to open this table and host an army of friends and family with food, stories, and laughter. We also pushed back the couches countless times to make room, not for the table, but for drum sets and guitars as flocks of troubadours gathered in that family room to express themselves through music.

## Guests

Henri Nouwen has a quote about hospitality that haunts me. In his book *The Wounded Healer*, he says it creates "an empty space where the guest can find his own soul."[1] It causes me to wonder what the

---

1. Henri Nouwen, *The Wounded Healer: Ministry in Contemporary Society* (Doubleday, 1972), 94.

space is and who the guests are. We can easily imagine that space as somewhere like our family room or maybe a kitchen table. But what if the space is more than a place? What if it's deeper?

Jesus didn't have a home on earth, a family room, a kitchen table of His own to offer, and yet throughout His time on earth, His call was, "Come to me, all who are weary . . . and I will give you rest."[2] His presence was the space. He opened His arms wide and invited all to find their souls in His company, or as Paul puts it, to "know what is the hope to which he has called you, what are the riches of his glorious inheritance in the saints, and what is the immeasurable greatness of his power toward us who believe."[3]

As I look at the gospel accounts, I see Jesus using every opportunity to invite people into His "space." Whatever was going on around Him, He found the hospitality in it. And a theme I've noticed in these opportunities is need. Sometimes, people were in need, and Jesus came to the rescue. Other times, it seemed that Jesus had the need. In either case, He took that need and turned it into a door that opened to the space where the guests could find their souls; they could find healing; they could, by His presence, be made whole.

Maybe I've picked up on this theme because I see it quite a bit in my own life. Born with a neuromuscular disease that puts me in a wheelchair, I've grown pretty familiar with the idea of need. Not a day goes by, maybe not even an hour, that I don't ask for help in some way. Walking is the least of my concerns. I need help with using the restroom, showering, getting dressed, turning over in bed at night, preparing food and eating it, opening doors, blowing my nose, scratching my head when it itches, grabbing a book from the shelf, and positioning my hands just right on a table so I can hold that book open to read it.

---

2. Matt. 11:28 NIV.
3. Eph. 1:18b–19.

Being so acquainted with need, I have often struggled, wondering if I am, more than anything else, a burden. There are only so many ways to ask for help before you start to wonder. Then I read about how Jesus asked a Samaritan woman for a drink of water, how another washed His dusty feet, and how His disciples gave Him something to eat after He rose from the dead. And through His needs, the people serving Jesus were served. Maybe need isn't actually a bad thing if we realize the hospitality of it. Maybe it can be a door that opens into spaces where, together, we find our souls.

## Loss and Connection

Our family room wasn't actually all that special. The stories and memories I have from that place are because of the people who have been there and the experiences we've shared. And so many of those experiences started with a need—a need for entertainment, rest, food, play, or fellowship. Those needs prompted a coming together, a making of time and space to not just meet, but to give all involved a glimpse into the Kingdom Come.

My most vivid memory in our family room happened just a few years ago in the middle of the night. I was awakened in my bedroom by a phone call, which also woke my dad across the hall. He came in to help me into my wheelchair and answer the call. My friend, on the other end, was crying and hysterical. Because my arms don't work well, I had to use the speakerphone. I didn't know yet what was going on, but I knew I needed to get to the other side of the house before I woke up anyone else. Groggy and lopsided in my chair, I rolled into our family room. My dad brought my phone in for me and set it on the table. I signaled him not to worry about turning on any lights, so he left me to it.

In the dark, my friend explained, sobbing, that a mutual friend of ours had committed suicide that evening. He gave me the few details he had, continuing to weep into the phone. I couldn't cry, though. I was in shock. I called someone else to confirm the information; then, I sat quietly for what seemed like forever. Darkness and loneliness swallowed me whole.

I don't know if Dad had left the room and just came back to check on me or if he had stayed nearby, listening and watching. Either way, as I sat in that black abyss, I felt his arms wrap around me. He held me as I trembled, as I said goodbye to the life I knew just minutes before, and stepped into a world that didn't make sense. Because of my need for help getting into my wheelchair, my dad knew what was going on. And because of my need to mourn, he and I encountered, more than ever before, what it meant to be father and son.

## The Room

I wonder what my six-year-old self would've thought had I known all of this was in store for the place where I sat and played. I imagine the neighbor stopping by to see the progress as Dad and I rested on the western corner of the foundation.

What if he had moseyed over, nodded at the hole in the ground, and told me I would laugh and cry with countless people in that room over the next thirty years? What if he had said I would write my first short story there or have my first kiss with the girl I would later marry?

I'm not sure the weight of it all would have registered with me. I'm not sure I could've grasped the joy, pain, and beauty of it. Then again, I'm not sure I can today. But I'm thankful for every bit of it, including that afternoon before the room was even a room. All that mattered to me as the sun set on our yard was that I was sitting with my dad, and one of those toy cars was going to crash and burn in the orange ravine below.

# CHAPTER TWO

# A Tightrope Walk

*from Kevan*

Being in a wheelchair, I'm probably the last person who should be using an acrobatics analogy, but here we go. We are looking at need and the attributes of hospitality that can be found in it. This whole concept is a tightrope walk, and on either side are drop-offs we too often fall into. On one side, we can see need as a burden: heavy, shameful, "too much." On the other side, we can see it as an idol: over-prioritized, all-consuming, even blinding.

Let's be clear and call these what they are. Both drop-offs are lies, Satan's twist on God's good work. And our acceptance of either lie as truth is a sin, which leads to death, whether emotional, relational, physical, spiritual, or all of the above. The enemy doesn't care as long as he breaks us and the world around us. It's important to be aware of these drop-offs—these lies—and to not miss, instead, the opportunities to walk together in the abundant life God intended for us.

## Burden

A few years ago, I was sharing a house with a couple of buddies, Ben and Matt. They both had day jobs outside the house, and I didn't like being home alone. So, here's what my routine looked like: A friend would come to the house in the morning to get me out of bed and ready for the day, and then I would "walk" by myself to downtown (about two miles through quiet neighborhoods) and spend most of my day working from there at a coffee shop. A few guys worked downtown who didn't mind helping me with the restroom, and at the end of the day, I'd "walk" home to spend the evening with roommates and other friends.

But sometimes, it was raining or too cold for me to make that trek to or from downtown by myself. Someone would take me in my van, or I would stay home. Sometimes, after a long day at work, my roommates would get a text from me asking for a ride home. And then there were the times when I was sick and needed extra care and attention, whether it was a cough or an upset stomach. Maybe I didn't sleep well the night before, or due to the weather, my body was just worn down more than usual, and I couldn't do as much or be left alone. And then what about when my friends were sick, or worn out, or had other responsibilities or crises of their own?

While Ben and Matt, as well as Evan, Ian, Isaiah, Damon, Steve, Joe, Drew 1, Drew 2, Drew 3, Drew 4, Wes, Nathan, Tyler, and a ton of other guys technically knew what they were signing up for and none of them ever complained, I felt some days like I might be asking too much. It's one thing to care for your own child, sibling, or parent, or even to be hired as a caregiver for someone with severe need. But these guys and I—we are connected by friendship. I'm a roommate, a coffee shop acquaintance, a fellow church member. It's one thing to ask for a door to be opened or even help with the restroom. But it's another thing when I get sick and need Ben to take the day off work to stay home with me, or instead of one restroom break at the coffee shop, my stomach freaks out, and I need Steve to help me with five restroom breaks in a row that are less than pretty to clean up. They were willing, but no one had really signed up for that depth of care, had they? Not for a buddy.

One morning, the guy who got me up was giving me a ride downtown, and these thoughts rolled around in my head. I was a burden. This way of doing things, this experiment of my friends taking care of me, was fun and maybe even revolutionary, but not sustainable. No wonder no one else in the disability world was doing it. Something had to change. These guys would be better off if they didn't have to care for me like this. Our friendships would be better off. Maybe I would be better off too.

Just then, I looked up to see a large building just two blocks from the coffee shop. An elderly man sat by the front door in a housecoat, smoking a cigarette. He greeted a hunchback woman in a wheelchair as she entered the building. A nursing home. I had seen it 100 times before and passed it twice that often. But I'd never really taken much notice. The thoughts rolling around in my head that day, though, placed a big, flashing neon sign over the building: "This is the other option!" The image stuck with me all day. It was a defeated image, the idea of living there, but maybe it was what I needed to do for everyone's sake.

That afternoon, when Ben picked me up, I mentioned the idea to him. I wish I could tell you his response was like a movie scene, with some epic monologue, or even a quip that has stayed with me for years since. I wish I could say that he looked me dead in the eye or slapped me in the face and told me to snap out of it. But he actually just kind of cocked his eyebrow, gave me a sideways look like I was crazy, and told me to stop, that I wasn't a burden. That was it, the whole talk. When we got home, we made a pizza and watched a movie together. And I have never again thought about living in a nursing home.

When we have a need, what is our posture? In the first place, are we willing to invite others into it? And then, if they do come in—whether we've invited them or not—how do we feel about our roles in the exchange? Do we feel like we owe them? Are we protective, reluctant, apologetic, self-deprecating, resentful? At my lowest, I have seen my need—and thus myself—as a hindrance to others' happiness and success. The narrative in my head is that I'm holding them back in life, and they would be better off without me. In a weird way, maybe I would be too. My view of the universe spirals, warps, and shrinks into a scared little worm as I bury my head in this destructive falsehood.

Whether we've had the label of "burden" placed on us by the words and actions of others or we've taken it up of our own accord, the root of that message is shame. And shame is the antithesis of what God intended us to experience as His creations. Jesus told a crowd in John 10:10 that He came to give us life abundantly. I can't help but picture a group of children running wild through an open field, playing, exploring, laughing—free. Life abundantly. But shame, according to Dr. Curt Thompson in *The Soul of Shame*, "will do everything it can to interfere with the emergence of joy, curiosity and the creativity that inevitably ensues."[1]

God created us to be communally adventurous, to live not just alongside one another, but *for* one another as well. And while He designed us to find a rich, full life within this kind of focus, Satan uses the tool of shame to disrupt that possibility. Looking through the lens of shame to see ourselves as a burden turns us inward and cuts us off from community, friendship, and fellowship. Dr. Thompson calls it "the inertia of shame," and he says the way we overcome it is to "turn in a posture of vulnerability toward someone else. . . . The very thing that has the power to heal this emotional nausea is the reunion of those parts of us that have been separated."[2]

---

1. Curt Thompson, *The Soul of Shame: Retelling the Stories We Believe About Ourselves* (InterVarsity Press, 2015), 53.
2. Thompson, *The Soul of Shame*, 34.

Seeing our need—and subsequently ourselves—as a burden is, unfortunately, an easy drop-off to fall into because if we're not careful, it can seem to prove itself. It doesn't take much to convince myself I'm a burden when I feel the quiver in my friend's arms as he picks up my deadweight. In a matter of seconds, my mind jumps from "I weigh too much" to "I am too much," and it's a pretty arguable point, especially if I leave it in my mind to bounce around for awhile by itself. But if I bring it into the light (in a conversation, for example), I might just find that my friend has a better argument against it than I do.

As Dr. Thompson says, the only way to counter shame is with vulnerability. It's the very thing our shame tells us we absolutely shouldn't pursue, but that's because vulnerability kills shame, so shame screams, "Stay away from that! It's terrible!" We demolish the burden narrative warping our heads and hearts by inviting others into our need. Unfortunately, some who get involved will feed the shame in us instead of fighting it with us. This is the way of the world, and those people will always come around, with or without help. But the right people, if given a chance, will flip on the light and scatter the darkness of shame. It's why I'm so thankful for friends like Ben, who counter my burden crises with a cocked eyebrow and a pizza. Because love, in word and deed, shatters lies if we let it.

## Idol

In college I was part of a church that met on Sunday nights, and we were just wrapping up for the evening. A group of us stood out on the sidewalk chatting and having a good time when it hit me that I had class the next day and had not touched base with my friend York, who always gave me a ride to school. I whipped out my phone and shot him a quick text telling him when to pick me up. His reply undid me. York texted back to clarify (strongly) that he wasn't a servant at my beck and call but a friend who helped out of love.

It may sound like an overreaction on his part. People send quick text messages all the time, and they are often crudely to the point: "Pick me up at 8." But I actually believe York was wise in his response, catching a spark before it burned down the forest. He saved me from a mindset that would have led me down some very lonely roads had it not been addressed at this point. My needs are numerous and ongoing. I've been blessed with a lot of amazing folks willing to meet these needs, and it could be easy to take advantage of this. If not checked, what is a gift could be mistaken for an entitlement. York saw in that little text interaction that I was losing sight of him as a person to love, and instead seeing him more as a tool to use.

Just as we can see need as a burden—either our own or someone else's—we can also fall into the drop-off of making need an idol. I have seen this far too prevalently in the disability community, under the guise of seemingly justifiable terms like "advocacy." Some well-meaning parents put up their dukes against teachers, doctors, airplane attendants, and other parents on behalf of their child's needs and then train these children to "self-advocate" in the same manner. And we see a similar trend in the able-bodied world as well, the Christian and secular mainstream alike, latching onto "self-care" as paramount to all other life choices while the Bible calls us to deny ourselves and take up our cross daily.[3] The needs may be different, but it's the same attitude that places our needs before anyone else's. In short, that heart says, "The world revolves around me."

It's a slippery slope because needs are meant to be shared. Whether obvious or subtle, need can tether us to one another by means of interdependence. But just like sharing prayer requests can easily slide

---

3. Luke 9:23.

into gossip, so can sharing our needs easily slide into selfishness. Our natural leaning is toward self-preservation, so to count others more significant than ourselves takes a conscious effort (via common grace), and to sustain it requires the Holy Spirit.

The first two of the Ten Commandments address idolatry. "You shall have no other gods before me," and then "You shall not make for yourself a carved image. . . . You shall not bow down to them or serve them."[4] More often than not, we like to ascribe idolatry to only things outside of ourselves. Ancient history puts stone or gold statues in our minds when we think of idols, while a modern take might be our cellphones, entertainment, celebrities, vices, or even being "in the know" at all times.

Whatever the idol is, we worship it, hold it in a place of esteem where only God should sit and reign, and give it full license to do with us as it pleases. We give it our loyalty. The person or thing we put there (God or idol) will consume us, shape our worldview, and ultimately dictate how we operate within that worldview. So, if we give that seat to God, we will have life, but if we set need in that place of highest honor, here's what the takeover looks like. Meeting that need will consume us. We will do anything to meet it and, at some point, expect others to do anything to meet it too. It will be the center of our universe, and we will operate as if it should be the center of everyone else's universe. Those around us or in our path will be no more than players in our game—tools or obstacles. Their needs will fade, and they will either whither or leave, and we will meanwhile waste away.

Instead of the abundant life, love, joy, and peace we find in Jesus, with need as our idol, we would experience frustration, fear, loneliness, and cortisol levels that will more than likely lead to a heart attack.

---

4. Ex. 20:3–5.

Satan will break us and the world around us. That is unless we have friends like York, who call it what it is—at a spark or a full-on conflagration—and help us refocus our priorities.

## The Same

While the analogy holds that seeing need as a burden or idol are two drop-offs on either side of the tightrope, at the end of the day, they are really the same fall. In both, we are putting need in the spotlight, and consequently barring ourselves and others from the life of fellowship that God created us to enjoy. In a noisy world of lies, we need to rehearse truth, hiding it in our hearts and reminding one another through word and deed. Vulnerability is key to this, and inviting one another into our needs can foster that connection—the kind we are all longing for. Instead of a stumbling block, let us discover need in its proper context and purpose, to bring us together and point us to Jesus.

# CHAPTER THREE

# Being a Hospital

*from Kevan*

Do you remember church potlucks in the 90s? They still happen, of course. But there was something unique and wonderful about those gatherings back then. I remember arriving early on Wednesday nights in the summer to eat before VBS or youth group. I guess they figured families were coming from work, daycare, and camps, and a meal would help relieve some of that midweek runaround stress.

The carpeted fellowship hall would fill up with kids playing tag between big, round folding tables, parents catching up with one another, and food. So much food. And this was the South, so whatever you have in mind when I say "So much food," double it. If you want to experience true Southern hospitality in full swing, find a time machine and go back to Welcome, North Carolina (look it up; it's a real place!) circa June 1996. But I didn't realize until more recently that on those Wednesday nights we were actually practicing hospitality in one of the purest and most public ways possible for our modern world.

## Etymology

To explore the concept of hospitality more in-depth, I asked my friend Jonathan Rogers to enlist the help of students from his Habit

Membership, a creative writing community based out of Nashville, Tennessee. Etymology is a brilliant kind of study that can tell us not just the history of a word itself but the history of whatever idea or thing that word represents. In this case, one of the Habit students, Tyler Rogness, came back with some intriguing observations on the root word for *hospitality*.

"[It seems] that prior to the thirteenth century," Tyler said, "there was a reciprocity being conveyed in the . . . word *ghos-ti*, which ultimately birthed both *host* and *guest*. . . . There was a richer communal dynamic at play in the ancient world."[1]

He went on to explain that the people who would have used the term *ghos-ti* in its original form and context were nomadic. They probably used it in reference to themselves and those they encountered in their travels. As their paths met with other nomads, each would share trades and goods the other might need. So then, who was the guest, and who was the host? I wonder if they would laugh at our delineation. To take it a step further, can there be a guest without a host or a host without a guest? Or, as Rosaria Butterfield puts it in her book *The Gospel Comes with a House Key*, "In radically ordinary hospitality, host and guest are interchangeable."[2] The two roles may be more inseparable than we are comfortable admitting.

Looking back at our church potlucks, this is what I see: *ghos-ti*. People came hungry, and they also brought food to share. The line between guest and host blurred, maybe even faded away altogether. Maybe some came hungrier than others, and maybe some brought more or less food than others, but we all showed up on the same level. It wasn't about only giving or only receiving, but a mysterious marriage of the two.

---

1. Tyler Rogness, email messages to Kevan Chandler, January 19 and 20, 2024.
2. Rosaria Butterfield, *The Gospel Comes with a House Key: Practicing Radically Ordinary Hospitality in Our Post-Christian World* (Crossway, 2018), 12.

In a world where hospitality has everything to do with entertainment and pomp and circumstance in our spotless houses, we gathered instead in a public place and brought macaroni, KFC, and a jug of sweet tea to enjoy together. I'm reminded of the early church in Acts:

> And all who believed were together and had all things in common. And they were selling their possessions and belongings and distributing the proceeds to all, as any had need. And day by day, attending the temple together and breaking bread in their homes, they received their food with glad and generous hearts, praising God and having favor with all the people. And the Lord added to their number day by day those who were being saved.[3]

They lived out hospitality with one another.

## Hospital Versus Hospitable

In his research, Tyler also noted that while *hospitality* is commonly defined as "the state of being hospitable," the word means, more precisely, "the state of being a hospital." It's a nuanced difference, but I like what Tyler had to say about this: "A hospital is simply 'a shelter for the needy,' and that's much more realistic than personally embodying the healthcare system." He went on to point out (with the help of Etymonline) that the Latin word from which *hospital* comes was not originally used to mean a building, per se, "but a quality of a person and their actions."[4] This ends us up back at the adjective *hospitable*, of course, but it's important to settle in for a moment with this idea of being a hospital.

Hospitals, as we know them today, have doors. We go into them

---

3. Acts 2:44–47.
4. Tyler Rogness, email message to Kevan Chandler, January 19 and 20, 2024.

to receive care. They also have ambulances, and back in the day, doctors did home visits to go out and provide care to those in need wherever they were. So, when I think of being a hospital as a quality of a person, I envision a lot of welcoming in and also going to. See how quickly the lines of giver and receiver blur? Likewise, it's easy to point out that those in need come into the hospital, but it's just as easy to realize those in need often can't get there, so the hospital goes to them. Coming and going are both the sick and the physicians. So it is that I've seen how the friend who comes to my house to get me up in the morning—to help me—may also be in need of care through companionship and conversation, which I can provide. He is a hospital coming to me; I am a hospital he comes to.

Another attribute of hospitals is their attentiveness. While I'm sure many of us have had differing experiences in doctor's offices and emergency rooms, the typical protocol (per the Hippocratic Oath taken by doctors) is that the hospital listens to our issues, observes our situation, and applies the appropriate plan to get us on the path to healing. We normally don't go in for a stomachache and come out with a cast on our leg. We get what we need because the hospital has paid attention to our needs and worked with us to meet those needs.

My friend Eric calls this aspect of hospitality a dance. More specifically, he says it's a dance between what I want and what they need. When he visits a family grieving the loss of a loved one, for example, he has ways he would like to care for them, but there may be other ways they would feel more cared for. What he wants may sometimes be a place to start, mind you, as long as he is open to what is really needed. If he swings in with what he thinks is best for them, even what will make him feel better in the situation, that family will end up with a cast on their leg. He also can't stand in the corner, twiddling his thumbs until the needy party tells him what to do. Instead, being a hospital means listening, observing, and participating in the care. We can invite others into our care or offer to join theirs. That's how dances work.

Lastly, hospitals are, in some senses of the word, generous. We live in a broken world and the healthcare system is no exception to that brokenness. But if a hospital operates like it's supposed to, our needs are usually met there without questions of whether what's required can be afforded by the hospital. If someone flatlines, a hospital will do all it can to revive them. If a transplant is needed, countdowns begin, and systems are scoured for a donor. There are blood drives and beds in hallways, life-flight helicopters and ambulances that roar to get patients where they need to go, and surgeons who fly in at all hours for specialized procedures. There are bills and insurance to deal with on the backend, but in the life-saving moments, hospitals, theoretically, don't take no for an answer.

As a hospital, how can I be generous in my approach to others? I can open my doors for them to come in, and I can go out to them. I can participate in their dance and even invite them into my own. Every life is precious, and I can have virtually no question of affordability in sustaining, preserving, or reviving it. And I can see value in each of these lives, recognizing that in every person, there may be something I can care for and something that can care for me. Or, as Chesterton would put it, "Every face in the street has the incredible unexpectedness of a fairy-tale."[5]

## Carolina Hospitals

So, in hot and sticky Welcome, North Carolina, circa June 1996, miniature hospitals played tag in a carpeted fellowship hall between big, round folding tables. And grown-up hospitals caught up with one

---

5. Gilbert Keith Chesterton, *Heretics* (John Lane Company, 1919), 63–64.

another while they set out dishes of food. Everyone showed up hungry, and everyone brought something for others to eat. Everyone sick; everyone a physician. Everyone dancing hospitality together.

We didn't know what we were doing beyond just getting together for church amid the busy week and trying to make sure everyone got fed in the process. That was about as far as we could see. Maybe some of the older hospitals knew better. But even at ten years old, if I didn't have words for it, I did still feel something. It was more than the summer air and freedom from school. We were living a full kind of life, and we were living it together. And it came with a peace not like the world offers, but a peace that makes your shoulders relax, your lungs fill up, and your face break into a smile when your best friend comes into the room. I like that peace, and as this hospital has grown up, I've come to understand what we were really doing there. We were putting on display, for all of Welcome and the world to see, a glimpse at the Kingdom of Heaven.

# CHAPTER FOUR

# Fluffy Road-kill

*from Kevan*

I t had been a nice, long day at the beach. A few days earlier, my band, Fluffy Road-kill, packed up our minivan in North Carolina and hit the road for a short "summer tour," having been invited to play at a friend's church in Fort Lauderdale, Florida. What was supposed to be a four-day road trip turned into a week. Our host said we could stay as long as we'd like, and none of us had responsibilities calling us home so soon. Our first year of college behind us, we figured we should jump at the chance while we had the time to spare.

We spent our days going to the beach and writing new songs in our host's living room. He kept the fridge stocked with orange juice and a full dish of jellybeans on the coffee table. The hot, sunny days were predictably cooled by hour-long thunderstorms rolling through around two o'clock every afternoon. And on this particular afternoon, I opted for some downtime by myself. Our host's grandson said he needed a haircut for work, and my bandmates volunteered to do the job in the driveway during the storm. You can see why I left them to it and retired to our bedroom at the back of the house.

The room usually belonged to our host's granddaughter, but she'd given it up for the guys and me to share. As rain pattered against windows, I rummaged through her CD collection. U2's album *How to Dismantle an Atomic Bomb* stuck out to me. I was more of a ska kid myself, but it was the only CD she had that was in English, so I gave it a try. I popped it into the little boombox, hit play, turned the volume down low to mix with the rain, and reclined my wheelchair for a nap.

I'm not sure how long I dozed, maybe three or four songs. The guys were still playing barbershop outside in the storm when I heard the front door crash open. Seconds later, my friend Zach burst into the bedroom. His shirt was soaked with rain, a wild grin spread across his wiry face. He halted dramatically in the doorway, his open hands before him like a surgeon. I looked at his hands, then back at his shirt, my foggy mind registering what I was looking at. Blood!

"Don't worry," he said, panting. "It's not mine."

Then he was gone, just like that, off to wash up, and I still wasn't fully awake yet. If it had been anyone else, I would have thought it was a dream. But that was Zach.

## Origin Story

I don't remember first meeting Zach. I do remember chasing each other through the hallways of the local Baptist church at VBS when we were about ten years old and then running into each other at concerts in middle school. In our respective youth groups, we were the two oddballs who went to the concerts, not to socialize but to actually see the shows and meet the bands.

In high school, Zach played bass for a local Christian heavy metal band called Zeteo. He was homeschooled, which meant he had a lot of time to read books and listen to music. He also had ADHD, which meant he had a profound amount of energy to read and reread those books and also teach himself how to play guitar by ear really, really well.

I don't remember meeting our other band member either, at least not the first time. Apparently, Danny and I went to preschool together, and I ran over his foot in the lunch line one day. That's his story, and he's sticking to it. But our paths crossed again in high school. Algebra class, to be exact. After class one day, I complimented his black T-shirt with a photo of the band P.O.D. on the front. Finally, a fellow Christian who likes rock music. I had found an ally. The next day, he was wearing a KORN T-shirt with the words "I have issues" scrawled across the back. *Oh boy*, I thought, *maybe I was wrong*. I started praying for his soul right away.

We went to a concert together shortly after, and I quickly learned that my first hunch was more accurate. We were enigmas to our podunk high school, as nice guys who loved Jesus and liked B-films and loud music. Everyone liked us, but no one knew what to do with us, so we stuck together and were soon best friends.

At one point in our eleventh-grade history class, an assignment came up to give a report on Ghandi. "Report" was a loose term in this instance, and I chose to write and perform a song. But the day arrived to give our presentations, and the guy who'd written the song with me was a no-show. Fortunately, though, his guitar was there—he had left it in the classroom after rehearsal a few days before—so I turned to my best friend for help. Danny played a little bit of guitar, enough for this project, anyway. During our lunch break, he swiped the guitar from the classroom and met me behind the basketball gym to figure out the song.

Twenty minutes later, we were pacing the hallway, waiting for our teacher to announce us like a rock band. (In case you were wondering, he was the coolest teacher ever.) As we walked into the classroom, I suggested we call ourselves Goat Cheese Cake. Danny shook his head, so I said the next thing that came to mind.

"How about Fluffy Road-kill?"

He looked over his shoulder at me and shrugged, "That'll work."

We played the song and the crowd went nuts, including our teacher. A few weeks later, we wrote two more songs—one about *The Scarlet Letter* for my English class and another about Oedipus for Danny's English class. By then, we'd returned the other guy's guitar to him, and Danny had started bringing his own to school. He played acoustic while I played the harmonica I got from my dad, and we both sang, though half of our set was more of an improv comedy act than an actual concert. At some point in there, our silly name took on meaning: alive (fluffy) in Christ, dead (road-kill) to sin. We recorded a few of our songs on cassette tape in the choir teacher's room before school one morning and shared them with friends. Word got around. Soon, teachers were writing us permission slips to play for their classes instead of attending our own.

Meanwhile, the rest of our time was spent going to underground Christian concerts. We had a thriving local music scene, with bands like Zeteo and countless others playing at churches, houses, and coffee shops within fifty miles every weekend. This is where we got to know Zach better, and he joined in on some of our favorite pastimes: Taco Bell, Bible study, and Christopher Walken movies. We even started going to Zeteo's rehearsals just to hang out and dance around.

Then, we took the leap out of just playing for our schoolmates. Fluffy Road-kill joined the scene. A goofy acoustic duo—long before Flight of the Concords made it acceptable—we opened for bands that played hip hop, punk rock, heavy metal, techno, and praise and worship. We just asked our friends if we could play with them, regardless of their genre, and they all said yes. Zach's band was at the forefront of letting us play with them, and soon, their hyperactive bass player couldn't help but grab a guitar and play along with us during our sets.

As our senior year came to a close, the duo was now a trio with

Zach fully on board. We had a CD and a decent following. But we were headed in different directions for college, which would make playing shows difficult. So, we decided to go all out for our last summer together, just one "tour" around North Carolina and Tennessee, and we'd put our all into it.

## Cords of Kindness

As we pulled out of the parking lot that July morning, my life changed forever. For eighteen years, I'd had a lot of friends but relied solely on my superiors for caregiving. My parents and parents' friends, pastors, youth pastors, teachers, school-appointed assistants, and even my big brother. I hadn't put much thought into it before, but until we got into our van and drove off, I had never had my peers take care of me like this.

The funny thing is, for as monumental of a revelation as that was, I don't think the guys and I really ever talked about it. There was no big "come to Jesus" talk about the weight of responsibility. We wanted to go on tour, and to do that, they had to help me with caregiving—so they did. Two guys my age—with no experience or training as nurses, dads, or babysitters—just a couple of wide-eyed Lost Boys, like me; "ragamuffins," Rich Mullins would've called us with a smile. Zach and Danny had no idea what they were doing, and for that matter, neither did I. We would just figure it out together, as friends do, and out on the open road, we had no safety net. It was just us—Zach, Danny, me, and my needs—for three days straight.

In the book of Hosea, the Lord reminds His prophet exactly how involved He is with His beloved creation. He says:

Yet it was I who taught Ephraim to walk;
I took them up by their arms,

but they did not know that I healed them.

I led them with cords of kindness,
    with bands of love,
and I became to them as one who eases the yoke on their jaws,
    and I bent down to them and fed them.[1]

In stories of kindness and friendship, it's often easy to focus our celebration on the act itself or the people involved rather than the Author of Kindness, the Father of Mercies.

Zach and Danny did an amazing job taking care of me that weekend as we stepped together into my needs. And it was the Lord at work all along the way, His cords of kindness leading us, as a group and individually. When Zach was twelve years old, he was a lonely kid, and Jesus, as he puts it, sat down next to him and said, "I'll be your friend." Danny grew up in the church, his dad being a pastor, but when he was fifteen years old, around the time we met in high school, he realized he needed and wanted to make his family's faith his own. And I grew up in the church as well, but when I was six years old, I had a lot of questions about eternity, and my dad introduced me to Jesus as the One I could spend eternity with. Because of these personal relationships with Jesus and His Holy Spirit living in us, our Fluffy Road-kill friendship has been what it is. It was because of His love for us that we could love one another in the first place; because of His presence—walking with us together and working in each of us— that we could see Jesus at the center of our friendship; and it was because we could see Him there that we had the capacity to love one another and accept love in return.

The experience turned my understanding of need and care upside

---

1. Hos. 11:3–4.

down to be intentional with a peer-to-peer caregiving approach. I now invite friends into my needs, for them to take care of me and me to take care of them. We each have unique needs and gifts, and we bring them all with us into this space of healing and growth. And it's the Holy Spirit living in these friends—and in me—who escorts us into deeper fellowship through the doors called need.

## After Tour

At one point on the road, Zach helped me in a public restroom. He paused, looked around, and said that until then, he'd never thought much about accessibility. Now, he was noticing new things everywhere. The restroom we were currently in, for example, was not particularly accessible. He said this as I lay on the linoleum floor, waiting to be put back into my wheelchair.

When we got home, Danny moved to Boone for school, but Zach and I were only twenty minutes from each other, so we continued to hang out regularly. That's actually an understatement. We were inseparable. You could inevitably find us at the local pub (which let us play the occasional concert), my parents' house, or his dorm since he now knew the ins and outs of my caregiving. I attended a tech school for music, but my time on Zach's campus, getting to know staff and student life, proved life-changing as well. Eventually, I transferred to John Wesley College, where he went. I worked toward a degree in counseling with a focus on prison ministry. Zach was long gone by then, off to Florida to pursue seminary and a young lady he had met along the way and later married.

On their wedding day, a few years later, I shared the story of Zach playing barbershop in the Florida thunderstorm. We all had a good laugh about it, but amid the goofiness and absurdity of that story, my takeaway was this: Zach came running, blood on his hands, because he wanted me to know what was going on. And while it would maybe have been more prudent to add the detail that our host's grandson outside was okay, Zach's instinct was to first and foremost let me know *he* was okay. In a moment of chaos, he knew I'd be concerned for his well-being, and he wanted, above all and maybe even subconsciously, to honor that. I wasn't just his subject of care, his project. He knew full well that I cared about him and for him too. This is our friendship, care for one another, a kind of two-way street, and an understanding of that between us.

By the end of the summer, we decided to keep the band going. We continued with shows throughout our college years, including a few more short tours, and still get together when we can to play music, just for fun. If our friendships weren't carved in stone before that first road trip, they certainly were after. Nowadays, Danny is married to his college sweetheart. They live in North Carolina with their two sons. Zach and his wife have three kids and live in Texas. He recently earned his PhD in Patristics, the study of the early church, and to my knowledge, he has never cut another man's hair since that one time in Florida.

# CHAPTER FIVE

# The Hospitality of Jesus

*from Kevan and Tommy*

J esus had needs. This is a concept many of us are probably hesitant, even scared, to entertain. By definition, God does not need anything. He is the Alpha and Omega, so profoundly that we can even refer to His "fullness," and it's from this very fullness that John says we receive "grace upon grace."[1] God's act of creation came from an abundance spilling over, not a lack to be filled. But when Jesus came as a man, He lowered Himself and took up the human element of need, something intimate to us and foreign to Him. Or was it?

Before we came along with our broken sense of need, God lived in triune perfection, a state of holy communion between the Father, Son, and Holy Spirit. It was out of this reciprocal love for one another that creation poured forth—the abundance mentioned above. In what is often called His High Priestly Prayer, Jesus said that He is in the Father and the Father is in Him.[2] He also explained to the crowds that He did nothing without the direction of the Father and told His disciples that the Holy Spirit was coming to be with them and that

---

1. John 1:16.
2. John 17:21.

the role of the Holy Spirit was to glorify Him.[3]

Maybe we don't call it need, as we understand it anyway. Perhaps we'd be more likely to call it coexistence or interdependence. Yet coexistence has a whole array of wrong connotations these days, and this triune perfection is more vibrant than interdependence. So words fall short, but there is something to the way the Trinity joyfully leans and feeds into one another that expresses a beautiful connection. It's unlike anything else, though perhaps seen through a glass darkly in our own human interactions, relationships, and dependence on one another. And it's into this sliver-like glimpse of that connection that Jesus stepped when He came to dwell with us. Let's say that communion wasn't foreign to Him, but need from lack was. So, He put on our broken and lacking sense of need like a coat, a part of the flesh He accepted to wear.

At the beginning of his gospel account, John says, "And the Word became flesh and dwelt among us."[4] An inherent trait of "flesh" is need, no way around that. To take on flesh, Jesus had to be wrapped in limitation, weakness, and vulnerability. Limitations did not limit Jesus, though, in fulfilling His mission to bring the Good News and be the Good News. His weaknesses, if you will, only served His purposes. The Man of All Sorrows held vulnerability as His own from birth to death and beyond, and every bit of it was for our sake.

Some of these needs were practical, like thirst and hunger, and by inviting others into them, Jesus healed the broken hearts of those involved. Other needs were more existential, with eschatological outcomes in their wake. And these examples that we read in Scripture are not exhaustive but a sample only. As John says at the end of his account, "Now there are also many other things that Jesus did. Were

3. John 5:19–20; John 16:13–14.
4. John 1:14.

every one of them to be written, I suppose that the world itself could not contain the books that would be written."[5] We make the same clarification here, that we've not pulled every example but just a few to share. Even as we write this, more examples jump out at us, and we have to say to each other, "Just focus on these for now."

But whether the needs Jesus experienced were common to man or particular to Him as the Messiah, His call with every need was to draw us to Himself. His every itch, every stomach growl, every odd request (a donkey?) were intentional and at His disposal for the redemption of mankind. By inviting the virgin mother, the woman at the well, and the fishermen all into His need, He healed them. His every need was an invitation, an open door for our lost and hurting world to step through with Him into salvation.

## Homeless

Jesus said He had no place to lay His head, but He didn't state this as a problem, per se.[6] It's in the context of fair warning to others who claimed a desire to follow Him "anywhere." He was telling them that the footsteps of following Him did not come with earthly plenty but, in fact, earthly lack. Of course, there is a spiritual bounty to be found walking in Christ's sandals, but He wasn't speaking in metaphor about some higher plane; He was speaking of a sober, plain reality. "I am making no promise of earthy comforts," He essentially said.

But you do have to wonder about the mind of Christ as He spoke so plainly. Do you imagine that He, at that moment, foresaw all the ways the needs for shelter, food, water, and rest would be met, often by someone else? Notice also in the Gospels that Christ sometimes used miraculous means to supply the needs of others—mainly wheat loaves

---

5. John 21:25.
6. Matt. 8:20; Luke 9:58.

and Galilean sea bass[7]—but He never used those same miraculous means to provide for Himself. Miraculous bread was even the key to Satan's first temptation in the wilderness. What was the miracle of Jesus not using the miraculous to meet His own natural needs? Was it just because Jesus, as a display of humility, would not consider equality with God a thing to be used for His own advantage? Paul speaks of this in the second chapter of his letter to the Philippians.[8]

But perhaps also, to meet His own needs, Jesus selflessly works through the means of others to offer them a taste of the joy found in meeting the needs of others. For everything, there is a purpose. There is nothing about the sovereign decree of God that is haphazard. Every need is a note or echo of the music that God wrote. Jesus didn't need anyone else, yet He chose to. And the reason for this deserves a closer look.

## High Priest

How can asking to be served be a service to others? This is what makes an exchange between Jesus and a Samaritan woman, along with a woman washing His feet and with His disciples feeding Him after His resurrection, so fascinating. In these encounters, instead of serving others, Jesus asked to be served, which may at first seem contrary to why He came. Jesus once also said of Himself, "The Son of Man came not to be served but to serve."[9] Was His mission statement just a memo for locust-eaters in the desert, or was the Kingdom of Heaven coming in ways we couldn't even begin to imagine? For "we do not have a high priest who is unable to sympathize with our weaknesses.... Let us then with confidence draw near to the throne of grace, that we may receive

---

7. We know there are only four types of fish in the Sea of Galilee, and none of them are sea bass, but it's fun to say, isn't it?

8. Phil. 2:6.

9. Matt. 20:28; Mark 10:45.

mercy and find grace to help in time of need."[10]

Need is a sermon that God purposed at the beginning of time, when He first commanded waters, shaped dirt, and grew fruit for food. In His sovereignty, He fashioned our needs to point us to Him. The Word who spoke everything into being stooped down to be born unto us and buried by us; to be thirsty with us, dusty, hungry. And by these needs, He quenched the thirst of the world, washed it clean, and offered it the Bread of Life.

---

10. Heb. 4:15–16.

# CHAPTER SIX

# Eternal Jesus
# Needed a Womb

*from Tommy*

I f we believe God came as flesh absolutely and truly, He had to come through the flesh naturally and completely. Jesus was conceived by the Holy Spirit, but He needed a knitted womb in which to be knitted. He had to be born to be with us. If instead of through contractions, blood, and pain, Jesus simply floated down to earth, a fully formed adult, from the first moment His toe gently alighted on the ground, His experience would have been fundamentally and drastically different. For that matter, so would ours.

Need is a fundamentally human trait, so in order to meet us as one of us, Jesus had to have fundamental needs. Breath, sleep, food, company, solitude, laughter, tears; the needs of the incarnate Jesus were inextricably tethered to our need for Him.

Ponder for a moment the inconceivable miracle of conception, a baby's immediate needs, and the miraculous means by which those needs are met. All life begins with the miracle of two becoming one in the womb. It is a miracle of the biological and mathematical. One of four hundred thousand opens up to one of one hundred million, and the life that God knew before the foundation of the world, in a flash, becomes a singular and unique body needing the singular and unique body of his or her mother.

Long before new life can sustain itself, it has to be sustained. A baby has to entwine and abide in the protection and sustenance inside the walls of his or her forty-week home. Moment by moment, this new life's very existence depends entirely on the selfless infusion of the mother's nourishment. She goes without to flourish the life within. And from the moment of birth, absolute dependency doesn't stop; it actually grows. The tender skin of a newborn needs the tender touch of the new mother; warmth, milk, song, and sway are the gifts given graciously to the life she holds and nourishes.

No baby has earned the sacrifice made by his or her mother. How can it be that the Author of Grace makes Himself so dependent upon it? This was the miracle of God, who needs nothing—He humbled Himself, stooping low beneath the demands of need. This is the miracle of the Opener and Closer of the Womb: He needed a mother, favored her, and received her favor.

And so, God met mankind as a man through the womb of a woman. From a lump of Jesus' hand-molded dust came Jesus as hand-molded dust. For our fallen minds to lay hold of eternal truth, it first required the eternal truth to lay hold of us. The incarnation of Jesus, God embracing flesh in the flesh, was precisely that: the Truth Himself (*the person*) laying hold of us. God, the absolute un-needing, came to a needy people and experienced need firsthand for the first time. In doing so, Jesus took the first step toward the rescue, resurrection, and re-creation of all things. Jesus, as a baby, was the next step in fulfilling a plan and keeping a promise.

To the deceiver of mankind, while the scent of forbidden fruit was still on the breath of the deceived, God made a promise: "I will put enmity between you and the woman, and between your offspring and her offspring; he shall bruise your head, and you shall bruise his heel."[1] Since humanity's deserved curse and God's perfect promise to undo that curse were both first proclaimed in the garden, we have known that the offspring of the woman would crush the head of her deceiver.

God promised the undoing of sin in the same breath that He pronounced the fallout of sin in Genesis 3:15. This is referred to as the *protoevangelium*, which means "first gospel." In time, God would stand in the place of man, and this was in order to bring glory to Himself. We are referring, of course, to the sacrifice of Jesus on the cross. Infallible God taking on the reality and consequence of fragile man. It was always inside the infinite mind of God for this to happen, so it needed to happen because God doesn't just know the future, He writes it. In Paul's letter to the Christians in Ephesus, we read a few simple words, "To the praise of his glorious grace."[2]

## Quite the "Ask"

Can you see the grace that was required for Jesus to need anything at all? Taking on a need is an act of grace itself. Have you ever asked someone for a favor? Asking for a favor is more profound than we may know. What we are doing, in essence, is asking someone to adopt a need as their own without any indebted reason. It wouldn't be called a "favor" if it was a "debt." We don't have to ask someone to pay a debt. But a favor? That implies we have no inherent right to ask for it. In other words, it would be the same as saying, "Hey, even though I have no right to ask, and you in no way owe it to me, by sheer gracious favor, might you . . . ?" Asking Jesus to suffer as our substitute would be quite the ask, but for God to have willed it before we even had the need to ask,

---

1. Gen. 3:15.
2. Eph. 1:6.

it leads me to not even know how to complete the thought, so I won't. Jesus taking on need is a vital thread in the tapestry of the gospel. A thread that, once woven, becomes the gospel and, if pulled, ruins it. I remember thinking as a child, "Sure, Jesus died for my sins, but since He's God's Son, I'm sure God kept it from hurting." Kids can have the best faith but the worst theology. A painless crucifixion of the Divine was not the greatest thought of my pediatric theological musings. But, in a way, it's a thought with which we grown-up, sophisticated, knowledgeable people must wrestle. To live in the flesh is to suffer in the flesh. Indeed, Jesus would not have been Emmanuel, God with us, if He had taken on a different flesh than we have. If the Father had somehow insulated His Son from the fragility and temptation of the flesh, He would have been simply donning a man suit to slink amongst the crowd unawares. That is the exclusive work of angels. Jesus did not come only in the image or appearance of a man but also in man's substance. The gospel is God incarnate, not God in costume.

The Good News that Jesus came to proclaim is the Good News that was ordained—it was always true in the will of God, but in the incarnation, Living Truth took on living flesh. Jesus, stepping in for the First Man, became the gospel in first person. Jesus being woven together in His mother's womb was truth in the abstract, becoming truth in the actual. Jesus being formed in the womb of Mary was the first and single greatest miracle of a life steeped in miracles. David pens in Psalm 139:

> For you formed my inward parts;
>> you knitted me together in my mother's womb.
> I praise you, for I am fearfully and wonderfully made.
> Wonderful are your works;
>> my soul knows it very well.

My frame was not hidden from you,
when I was being made in secret,
    intricately woven in the depths of the earth.[3]

Jesus needed a womb of flesh to be woven in as flesh. And the be-
trothed virgin Mary from Nazareth was chosen. The angel's unbeliev-
able-yet-believed words and Mary's humble and humbling response
are both recorded in the first chapter of Luke's gospel:

> The angel said to Mary, "Greetings, O favored one, the Lord is
> with you. . . . Do not be afraid, Mary, for you have found favor
> with God. And behold, you will conceive in your womb and bear
> a son, and you shall call his name Jesus. He will be great and will
> be called the Son of the Most High . . . and of his kingdom there
> will be no end."
>
> And Mary replied, "How will this be, since I am a virgin?"
>
> The angel answered, "The Holy Spirit will come upon you,
> and the power of the Most High will overshadow you; therefore,
> the child to be born will be called holy—the Son of God . . . For
> nothing will be impossible with God."
>
> And to this, Mary said, "Behold, I am the servant of the Lord;
> let it be to me according to your word."[4]

"Let it be." If you read the entire exchange in Luke 1, you will find
that Mary had some fear and confusion mixed in there at times. Yet her
immediate response to God's Word wasn't hedged with a list of con-
ditions or a reflex of pride, but the very essence of humble obedience:
"Let it be." In other words, in response to God's most unbelievable

---

3.  Ps. 139:13–15.
4.  Luke 1:26–38, paraphrased.

will, her simple response was, "Amen," and she was blessed for it. A simple, sweet, fragile girl carried in her teenage belly for nine months not just *a* life—precious and priceless as that would be in itself—but she carried *the* Life and Light of Man.[5]

## Knitted to Need

We needed Him, so in order for that need to be met, Jesus had to need like us. As the author of Hebrews writes, "He had to be made like his brothers in every respect, so that he might become a merciful and faithful high priest in the service of God, to make propitiation for the sins of the people."[6]

In order for Jesus to take man's place on the cross, He took on man's flesh to absorb God's wrath in justice. His veins coursed with fragile blood, yet His heart still beat with purity. His ears endured unstained the deception of the dust-bellied serpent and rebuked the creature's divided tongue with the Word rightly divided. He humiliated His infiniteness by enrobing it in our weakness. Christ, the Divine, became the vine, the same living substance of the orphaned branch, and grafted the needy branch to Himself, adopted, like the conceived and helpless child is grafted into the mother and nourished.

We needed Jesus, so Jesus needed a womb, and Mary said, "Let it be."

---

5. John 1:4.
6. Heb. 2:17–18.

# CHAPTER SEVEN

# The Intentionality of Need

*from Kevan*

Need is not a sin, just as much as a broken leg or a torn shirt is not inherently evil. Jesus Himself referred to need as a tool when the crowd asked Him about a blind man.

"Who sinned here?" they asked Jesus. "This man or his parents, that he is blind?"

"Neither," He replied. "But so that the works of God might be displayed in him."[1]

Need itself wasn't a result of the fall but fell along with the rest of creation when sin entered the world. It was meant to be yet another beautiful picture of God's love for us. And while it now causes pain and is associated with hardship, need can still point us back to Him in His sovereignty and grace, just as He intended it to from the beginning. In an abundance of power, imagination, love, and glory, God spoke the universe into being. And in the process, He divinely designed His creation to function with need. The first suggestions of

---

1.  John 9:1–3, paraphrased.

this come in the creation story, right at the beginning of Genesis, long before the fall occurred.[2]

On the third day of creating, God said, "Let the earth sprout vegetation, plants yielding seed, and fruit trees bearing fruit in which is their seed, each according to its kind on earth."[3] He made fruits and vegetables to need seeds for continuing their existence, and those seeds needed homes to protect them before their time came to reproduce. This vegetation, whether tree, bush, or root, would also come to provide food for "everything that has the breath of life."[4]

The next day, He created lights in the sky (the sun and moon) and commanded, ". . . Let them be for signs and for seasons, and for days and years, and let them be lights in the expanse of the heavens to give light upon the earth."[5] He set up the sun and moon to mark time, but He's outside of time, so who was it for? The rest of creation, and especially us, two days before we were even made!

On the fifth and sixth days, He created animals to populate the sea, sky, and land accordingly and made man. And not only did He make all these things to need food and time, but He also made fish to need the sea, birds to need the sky, and beasts and man to need the dry land. Each of His creatures has its own ecosystem it needs to survive and flourish. He intentionally made us this way and spent the first four days specifically preparing those ecosystems for us to depend on and enjoy.

Finally, He saw that the man was alone and said that just wouldn't do. Adam needed a wife, a companion, and someone to share his load and life with, so God gave him Eve. And every step of the way, as He formed and fashioned these needy things, God looked at them at the

---

2. Gen. 1:11–2:25.
3. Gen. 1:11.
4. Gen. 1:30.
5. Gen. 1:14–15.

end of each day and said, "It is good." It would seem He doesn't just put up with need but actually delights in it.

## Babies

Jesus kicks off His famous Sermon on the Mount with the Beatitudes, and the first four of these harken back to need and vulnerability:

> Blessed are the poor in spirit, for theirs is the kingdom of heaven. Blessed are those who mourn, for they will be comforted. Blessed are the meek, for they shall inherit the earth. Blessed are those who hunger and thirst for righteousness, for they shall be satisfied.[6]

And later, He reiterated this when people brought their children to see Him.

Jesus was playing with some kids, and the disciples didn't get it or like it. They scolded the children—and their parents—for bothering Jesus. And Jesus retorted, "Let the little children come to me, for theirs is the kingdom of heaven. And by the way, you could learn a thing or two from how they come."[7] But Luke's account gives a little extra note that we should be careful not to gloss over too quickly.

At the beginning of the account, Luke says, "Now they were bringing even infants to Him."[8] This stops me in my tracks because I actually have a lot of infant-like qualities in the scope of my own personal needs. I am an adult. I'm married. I pay taxes. I can do math in my head, read G. K. Chesterton and understand (most of) it, and buy airplane tickets. But I still need others to bathe me, dress me, sometimes feed me, and always help me use the restroom. If I'm not in my wheelchair,

---

6. Matt. 5:3–6.
7. Luke 18:16, paraphrased.
8. Luke 18:15.

I literally can't move or hold myself upright.

Usually, when I read this scene in Matthew, Mark, and Luke, I imagine wiry kids around eight or nine years old, barefoot with dirt behind their ears. A whole bunch of them come running and dogpile themselves onto Jesus. He's laughing, wrestling with them, playing tag, or telling them stories on His knee, their eyes wide with wonder. And I don't doubt that this happened, too, but Luke's account is specifically about newborn babies. And newborn babies can't do much at all.[9]

So often, our analogy is that we should come to Jesus like kids come up to their parents, trusting them to provide wisdom, safety, comfort, care, nourishment, etc. And there is truth to this. But we're still talking about a child walking up, tugging on his dad's pant leg, looking up, and asking for these things. Whether we realize it or not, we tend to assume a bit more works-based faith in our walk with the Lord than we might realize or care to admit. What about when we can't walk up to our dad? What about when we are at the end of our strength and can't even reach out to touch the hem of Jesus' garment? What about when our shame won't let us look up into His eyes and ask? As someone with a disabled body and an equally disabled soul, I am in desperate need of a Rescuer coming to get me more than a home plate to run to (for all you baseball fans out there).

A group of guys lowered their crippled friend through a roof to get to Jesus, and Jesus commended their faith. He sidled up next to a lame beggar by a pool and offered, unprompted, to heal him. And as He cradled a newborn baby in His carpenter arms, He essentially said to His disciples, "If you don't approach the Kingdom like this, you won't get in."[10] I find comfort in this, that He calls us to "come"

9. As a fun pro-life side note, the Greek word *brephos* that Luke uses he also uses in Luke 1:41 when referring to John the Baptist in utero.
10. Luke 18:17, paraphrased.

as helpless as a newborn baby, not even big enough or strong enough to crawl, carried to Him or found by Him, our total deadweight held in His arms because we can't help at all. We just curl up there, yawn, gurgle, coo . . . and rest.

## Invitation

The root of our need is for the presence of God. Just as He set up ecosystems for His creation to thrive in and designed children to need their parents, these and our other needs are actually just subsidiary reflections of our deeply built-in reliance on Him. This need—the big one—was met organically early on in the garden. But with the fall came a separation, a severing of that communion and the need being naturally met in such a concrete way. The story of all creation since then has been to get back there, to that ultimate need being met by God with us, which Jesus came to make possible again. And our more finite needs—the weights and worries of the world—point us to that ultimate need and the One who can meet it. They did before the fall, by design, and they do so now, much to Satan's chagrin.

So, if our needs point us to God, why can't they point others to Him as well? Every need points us back to God's love and our great need for Him, and one of those "sub-needs" that God imbued us with is our need for one another. It only stands to reason, then, that our need for one another can not only point us to Him, it can point others to Him as well. In their book *Safe People*, Dr. Henry Cloud and Dr. John Townsend point out, "God doesn't create us to be relationally self-sufficient. He loves us to need each other. Our needs teach us about love and keep us humble. True self-sufficiency is a product of the Fall."[11]

And again, in *The Wounded Healer*, Nouwen right-hooks us with

---

11. Dr. Henry Cloud and Dr. John Townsend, *Safe People: How to Find Relationships That Are Good for You and Avoid Those That Aren't* (Zondervan, 1995), 127.

a hard truth to consider: "Hospitality is the ability to pay attention to the guest. This is very difficult, since we are preoccupied with our own needs, worries, and tensions, which prevent us from taking distance from ourselves in order to pay attention to others."[12] And it seems to me that this is the exact opposite of what we should be doing. Rather than our needs distracting us or deterring us from hospitality, they should actually be our greatest tool to accomplish it. They should open us up to profound opportunity. Our needs drop us into a tunnel vision, either toward self-pity or glorious light. If we choose the latter, it's a sight unlike any other to see.

A few years ago, some friends and I were hiking part of the Great Wall of China. A lot of the wall has been restored and reinforced for the safety of its millions of tourists visiting each year. But there are some areas that have not yet been worked on, and these areas are barricaded by a short wall and a sign discouraging entry. As you can imagine, that "discouragement" acted as more of a challenge and encouragement to our group of thirty-something-year-old guys looking for adventure. We climbed over the barricade and set out to traverse a crumbling wall that had been built around the time of Jesus.

It was a treacherous climb. My friends carried me in a backpack and held onto each other for stability as we, at times, navigated two-foot-wide boulders with 100-foot drop-offs on either side. Sweat soaked our shirts, and blisters covered our feet and hands as we gasped for breath in the ever-thinning air with every step upward. And we did all of this because Tom, the most ornery member of our team, had run ahead earlier and come back to report. It would be a lot of work, uncomfortable, even dangerous, but he said this push to our limits would prove worthwhile. And it did. We reached a plateau and looked out

---

12. Nouwen, *The Wounded Healer*, 89.

over a daunting world. Nowhere else on earth could give you this grand a view. Miles of rolling, roaring, ruling green masses of land, forest, and rock, as far as the eye could see, and we were looking down on all of it.

As our needs lead us into the presence of our Lord, as He always intended, let us bring others with us by inviting them into those very needs. By divine design, He is calling us back to Himself, and it's where we're all longing to be, anyway. We have the road to get there; we know the way and have traveled it. We are traveling it. It's unconventional and often uncomfortable, but the view will prove even more worthwhile than the Great Wall of China.

Come and join me as children—in weakness, vulnerability, and need, "so that you too may have fellowship with us; and indeed our fellowship is with the Father and with his Son Jesus Christ."[13] I want you to see the wonderful glory of God that I get to see from here, curled up in His arms.

13.  1 John 1:3.

# CHAPTER EIGHT

# While in Prison

*from Kevan*

Near the end of my time in college, I took an internship with a prison ministry in Arkansas. Thirty-some years earlier, Chuck Colson was part of Nixon's Watergate scandal and went to prison for it. While in prison, he found Jesus, and his life was radically changed. When he got out, he started a ministry called Prison Fellowship to serve inmates and their families.

At the time of my involvement in Prison Fellowship, there was a special branch of the ministry called InnerChange Freedom Initiative. A few months before their release, inmates were invited to go through a program centered around preparing them for the outside world. Those who joined moved to a separate building on the prison grounds for their last few months to go through intensive courses and community living. We provided Bible studies, as well as classes on growing in work ethic, family values, financial stewardship, and a Christian worldview. Arkansas' prison system was a flagship for this experiment, and I had the honor of being part of it for the summer before my senior year.

Today, hanging in my study is a picture of Butch Cassidy and the

Sundance Kid. The two bandits hold worried expressions in a shadowy charcoal rendering. If Robert Redford walked in, he'd think he was staring at a black and white mirror. I got it from one of the men I worked with in the program. He was in his late forties when I met him and had only recently discovered the natural talent hidden somewhere in his bones.

His artwork teaches me some key truths about life. First, people change. My friend went from being a thief to being an artist, and a good one at that. Second, what seems like an unfortunate situation is sometimes actually for the best. My friend would never have known he had this gift if he hadn't been caught and done time. I look at that picture, and I think not just of his abilities as an artist but of the new heart he got when he gave his life to Jesus, which also may not have otherwise happened. It's a beautiful story of redemption and grace, and I love being reminded of it like this every day. I need the reminder just about that often.

When I look at the picture of Butch and Sundance, though, I think not only of my friend who drew it. Memories flood in of all the guys I got to know that summer. There were 120 of them, and every one had a story of his own to tell of redemption. In the two months I spent there, I got to watch firsthand as life came back into the eyes of men who had lost hope. I got to see hard men weep and joke with one another like kids as we let the Holy Spirit soften us. And I got to witness greed, pride, and selfishness melt away as we each surrendered to the Lord and put the brothers around us before ourselves.

## That Summer

I had some strange mishaps that summer. The door to my handicap minivan came off its track at one point, and its muffler fell off another time, just to name a couple. The last week of my time there, I thought we were surely in the clear. Nothing else could possibly go wrong, and the finish line was just up ahead! That's when it started raining. Maybe that's an understatement. We had an apocalyptic downpour, a good old-fashioned Southern summer storm. It was the kind that's so massive and relentless that you begin to wonder if this is how it will be from now on. Gray, as far as you can see, and rain until Jesus comes back. But I had a job, so I showed up for work.

The prison was huge. While our program had 120 guys enrolled, the campus held about 900 altogether. To get to our building at the very back of the property was no small feat.

My morning began each day with checking in at the front gate. I passed through a barbed wire fence and entered a small brick room, where I got thoroughly patted down. Security leafed through my Bible every day, without fail, just to make sure. From there, I was dismissed and crossed a covered walkway to the main building, an enormous cinder block construct, several stories tall, packed to the gills with inmates and guards. Inside, I navigated the block of multi-floored cells to a back door.

Exiting the back door, I came out onto an open space. A wide concrete pad with a handful of picnic tables overlooked an all-purpose athletic field. To the left, a narrow, uncovered paved path stretched 150 yards to another gate with a guard posted. I greeted him every morning as he unlocked that gate to let me in. Then a final strip of thin outdoor pavement took me to the door of our building, a one-level warehouse with rows of cots and a couple of classrooms—the epitome of community living.

On a sunny day, as most days were in June and July, it was a warm and pleasant walk with nothing to worry about but some early morning mosquitoes. But that last week of my stay, the rain came down and changed everything. I bolted from the car, through the gate, and into the small brick room, already drenched. At the end of the covered walkway, I entered the main building and shivered, industrial AC hitting my wet clothes. And the worst was yet to come.

As the back door opened, I readied myself like Benny "the Jet" Rodriguez in *The Sandlot*, cracking my knuckles and steeling myself for the run of my life. I burst into the pouring rain and veered to the left, toward the gate to our building. The guard was ready to welcome me in, so I didn't have to slow down. I tore past him and headed down the homestretch, the door now in sight through what felt like a waterfall. My wheelchair cut like a knife through puddles six inches deep, splashing up water all around me. Adrenaline raced through my veins and motors, all as one, as I flew toward the double doors of our building. Familiar faces threw open both doors for me, and I coasted into the warehouse, sliding to a stop on the concrete floor.

I was instantly surrounded by a congregation of white jumpsuits, the attire for inmates here. Guys I had served all summer, teaching and counseling, came around me with piles of fresh towels to dry off my body, clothes, and machine. Men convicted of assault gently dried my hair and face and bent down to warm up my legs. Former drug dealers sopped up the standing pools on my armrests and seat. They loaned me a white jumpsuit while my clothes dried, joking that the guards wouldn't let me out at the end of the day.

I sat there for at least a half hour, my wheelchair turned off, accepting their care for me, just inside the front doors. As they finished using the last towel on my footrests, I thanked my friends and powered up my wheelchair. My mind was already on the next thing: class lectures, counseling sessions, Bible studies, chess matches, and conversations. We had a busy day ahead of us, and just a few more of them before I would be gone, so we had to make the most of it.

"You guys ready for class?" I asked as I leaned into my joystick to turn.

But nothing happened. My wheelchair didn't move. I looked down for the first time to realize the screen was blinking. The motors were not engaged. Maybe one of the manual switches was bumped during the drying process. I had them check the switches. Everything was in place as it should've been. I turned it off and back on, but still nothing. I pushed the joystick every which-a-way, but the motor wouldn't click, and the wheels wouldn't budge. We eventually decided that the inner workings of the wheelchair were waterlogged and just needed time to dry out, but none of us knew exactly how long that should or would take.

For the next four days, I was fully dependent on society's outcasts. As a counselor in a prison, I never thought my summer would involve mediating arguments between inmates over who would be next in line to push my 350-pound wheelchair. Putting it in manual, the guys took turns moving me from classroom to office, back and forth, and everywhere in between, all day. If I were sitting still for a class or social time with them, some would take the liberty of tinkering to see if they could fix the mysterious problem.

Once, I was playing chess with someone while a man with a mustache lay on the floor behind me. He was taking apart one of my motors to examine it. I asked him, half joking if he had any idea what he was doing.

"I think so," he answered with a laugh. "A motor is a motor. It can't be all that different from the ones I used to steal off cars."

## Deed and Truth

What was a state of helplessness for me became an opportunity for my friends and me to grow. The program we offered introduced these guys to Jesus, His teachings, and a new life of integrity and character. We learned together how to "do nothing from selfish ambition or conceit, but in humility count others more significant than your-selves,"[1] as Paul puts it, and as John says, to "not love in word or talk but in deed and in truth."[2] And suddenly, we had a chance to put it all into practice.

When we are in "survival mode," as crime and prison cultures tend to foster, we are on high alert for self-preservation. We don't want to get caught or hurt or misunderstood again. We sleep with one eye open, stow away an extra biscuit at lunch, and throw the first punch before the other guy can. The part of our brain that says "eat, run, fight" is in charge and pulls all the resources of our body and attention to itself, shutting off the other parts of our brain that are creative, silly, and selfless. Survival mode strips away all the fun stuff in the name of just not dying. And robbing a bank, or being locked in a building with 900 other people who have robbed banks (or worse), will put you squarely in the heart of this mindset.

So, when Jesus shows up in that prison and tells us to put others before ourselves, imagine how radical that is! It's radical for anyone, but for those living in what psychologists call our "downstairs brain" (survival mode),[3] it's practically impossible to consider. In that level of stress, all we are wired to think about is what's best for ourselves, nearly blind even to the needs or cares of others.

Nearly.

God designed us to have chemical reactions that kick in when we find ourselves in dangerous situations, but He also embedded in us a seed called love. It's a seed buried deep and brought forth to bloom by the work of His Holy Spirit and the factors He places around us to

---

1. Phil. 2:3.
2. 1 John 3:18.
3. Daniel J. Siegel and Tina Payne Bryson, *The Whole-Brain Child: 12 Revolutionary Strategies to Nurture Your Child's Developing Mind* (Random House, 2012), 38–41.

draw it out. These factors are often relationships and the needs of those we care about. It can jar us out of inward focus and move us toward growth and healing as we turn our attention to serving others.

My friends and I had gotten to know each other over the summer, praying and studying Scripture together, telling jokes, and talking about life. We had delved deeply into heart matters and reconstructed our ways of thinking. Most of what we worked on was preparation, or "theory," in a way. How will I love my wife when I get out? How will I nurture my kids? How will I commit to my job and work hard? In prison, we could work on submitting to authority and loving our neighbor, to an extent, but even those things looked different in that culture than they would on the outside. But we did a lot of talking together, a lot of work, and a lot of play, which all, with time, built a bond between us. And then a need arose.

My wheelchair had stopped working, and after two months of life together, these guys really knew what that meant. They knew it to their core, where that seed lay quietly, ready to spring up. Kevan couldn't move, and he was usually bouncing all over the place. He usually met with this person over here, then taught this group over there, then played chess with these folks over here, then did paperwork there, then facilitated this meeting over here. They saw the gap and the needs of someone they cared about and stepped in to help. The internal work turned outward, allowing hands and feet the opportunity to act upon what hearts had been learning all summer. Our theory of how to love one another took on flesh and became a reality for us to grow in and flourish.

## Young Men

The last day came. My wheelchair was still waterlogged and unresponsive. We had a general assembly with everyone in the program, and then we were dismissed for the day. Saying my goodbyes, I looked around at a small remnant of guys who especially weren't ready to see me go. I wasn't ready either.

I asked one in particular to push me across campus to the exit. He was my age, a kind soul whose summer had started in darkness and ended up brighter than the Southern sun. He had given his life to Christ, and we had studied 1 John together because it felt like John had written it to us: "I write to you, young men, because you are strong, and the word of God abides in you, and you have overcome the evil one."[4] I had watched as his eyes went from gray to blue and a smile found its way to his face, all because of Jesus and the wonder of forgiveness.

He took me as far as he could go, and we didn't say much, but I cherished every moment of it. The sun was out, and the rain was long gone. The only sign that it had ever been there was a young man in a white jumpsuit pushing another young man in a broken-down wheelchair. I remember a distinct feeling like I was on a walk with a saint. The prison faded around us. We were strolling through a park, as old friends, brothers, free, loving one another in deed and in truth.

I got home to North Carolina two days later, and my chair turned on just fine.

---

4. 1 John 2:14b.

# CHAPTER NINE

# The Fountain
# Needed a Drink

*from Tommy*

How can the thirst of a Savior become the salvation of a sinner? John's gospel recounts the occasion of a thirsty Jesus sitting by a well. His lips dry, tongue sticking to the roof of His mouth. It's hard to imagine God being "wearied . . . from his journey," but here He is.[1] His disciples went into town to get food, but Jesus hung back. He'd rest and wait for them to return with lunch. When a local woman came to collect water, Jesus said to her, "Give me a drink."[2]

That is certainly one way for the Creator to begin a conversation with His creation! The woman was shocked. "How is it that you, a Jew, ask for a drink from me, a woman of Samaria?"[3] So far, this woman knew only two things about Jesus: He's a man, and He's Jewish. According to the culture, men did not address women socially. And Jews definitely did not, under any circumstances, associate with Samaritans. These were social chasms that couldn't and shouldn't be crossed. Little

---

1. John 4:6.
2. John 4:7.
3. John 4:9.

did she know, there was a much larger chasm at play here, and God in the flesh was crossing it to reach her.

But there was actually a third thing she also knew about Jesus: He was thirsty. And while His masculinity and ethnicity separated Him from her, even elevated Him above her to a point she couldn't reach, His thirst did the opposite. It made Him relatable—everyone gets thirsty—and to go further, it made Him lower than her, in a sense. He needed her help. She had the water. He asked her for it. In a culture and life where she was usually treated as less than, Jesus invited her to stand above for a moment. He gave her the authority to pull Him up out of the ditch of thirst. And so, walls came down, maybe still brick by brick as the conversation went on, but this was an important first brick.

## The Conversation

Can you imagine if Jesus tried to spark up the conversation any other way? "So, you like water too, huh?" What if He had opened with one of the other lines that He used later on? "Everyone who drinks of this water will be thirsty again,"[4] or "True worshipers will worship the Father in spirit and truth,"[5] or especially that bit about her five husbands—that wouldn't have gone well!

As best as we can read it, she was a tough woman on the outside and a scared little girl on the inside. Jesus had to slip past the first while not terrifying the second. So, He asked her for a drink of water. He related to her. He stooped down to her. He even, in a way, submitted to her for her sake and, ultimately, her salvation. And she couldn't believe it.

I can't help but wonder if Jesus smiled as He answered her question: "If you knew the gift of God, and who it is that is saying to you,

---

4. John 4:13.
5. John 4:23.

'Give me a drink,' you would have asked him, and he would have given you living water."[6]

"Sir," the woman said, "you have nothing to draw water with, and the well is deep. Where do you get that living water? Are you greater than our father Jacob? He gave us the well and drank from it himself."[7]

Jesus explained, "Everyone who drinks of this water will be thirsty again, but whoever drinks of the water that I will give him will never be thirsty again. The water that I will give him will become in him a spring of water welling up to eternal life."[8]

"Sir," she said, "give me this water, so that I will not be thirsty or have to come here anymore to draw water."[9]

The woman simply could not comprehend a thirst beyond the sweat and shame of the midday well, not for a failure of intellectual assent but for the lack of a heart able to embrace something beautiful outside of the pre-worn paths of her understanding and experience. And a new heart might just be what she would pull from the well this day.

Their conversation continued as Jesus said to her, "Go, call your husband, and come here."[10]

When she answered, "I have no husband." Jesus replied, "You are right in saying, 'I have no husband,' for you have had five husbands, and the one you now have is not your husband. What you have said is true."[11]

Shocked again, the woman said, "Sir, I perceive that you are a prophet."[12] Then she figured, "Hey, it's not every day I chat with a

6. John 4:10.
7. John 4:11, paraphrased.
8. John 4:13–14.
9. John 4:15.
10. John 4:16.
11. John 4:17–19, paraphrased.
12. John 4:19.

prophet," and so she asked a question she had probably wondered about for a while: "Our fathers worshiped on this mountain, but you say that in Jerusalem is the place where people ought to worship."[13]

Jesus liked answering honest questions from thirsty people. "Woman," He said, "believe me, the hour is coming when neither on this mountain nor in Jerusalem will you worship the Father. You worship what you do not know; we worship what we know, for salvation is from the Jews. But the hour is coming, and is now here, when the true worshipers will worship the Father in spirit and truth, for the Father is seeking such people to worship him. God is spirit, and those who worship him must worship in spirit and truth."[14]

The woman said to Him, "I know that Messiah is coming (he who is called Christ). When he comes, he will tell us all things."[15]

She knew that the Messiah was coming. And although she couldn't quite imagine exactly what this man was referring to, she knew enough to know that once the Messiah did come, so would the answers.

And to this, plainly yet miraculously, Jesus declared, "I who speak to you am he."[16]

## Changed

Imagine the dramatic pause this statement would cause. Peer with me through the well like a keyhole into a woman's heart at that very moment when the words of a stranger became the Living Word. Can you see her face? Her snappy tongue suddenly became as still as her eyes were wide. Her broken Samaritan heart contemplated the seed of a thought she didn't know she could think, a flower of wonder that started

---

13. John 4:20.
14. John 4:21–24, paraphrased.
15. John 4:25.
16. John 4:26.

to grow up through a crack. And there was only one way for her to respond to what He'd just said. Scripture recounts next that she left her water jar and ran off into town, saying to everyone around her, "Come, see a man who told me all that I ever did. Can this be the Christ?"[17]

Notice, at the beginning of their interaction, the Samaritan woman called this mysterious Jew "sir," which is the Greek word *kyrios*. It denotes respect and authority, as it does in English. As they continued to talk, "sir" gave way to "prophet" before flashing to "Messiah." At that point, she clearly didn't see Jesus as just a kind and captivating—albeit parched—stranger. Perhaps the living water was already on its way to her calcified heart. Then, as she dashed off to town, the title of "Christ" spilled from her heart onto her lips and out into a dry and thirsty world.

Upon their return, Jesus told His disciples, "I have food to eat that you do not know about. . . . My food is to do the will of him who sent me and to accomplish his work."[18] He even went on to say, "Lift up your eyes, and see that the fields are white for harvest."[19] He was satisfied, filled, as if He'd already eaten, excited about deeper things than a sandwich from the market: grace, salvation, and the Kingdom of Heaven moving in. And a facet, in this particular circumstance, of His work was to have need and invite someone into it. The fields were ripe for picking, He said. A woman at the well of Jacob was ready for harvest, and Jesus did the will of His Sender by being thirsty and asking this dear, ready woman for a life-changing drink.

Jesus, in asking for a favor at her well of labor, had the opportunity to reveal Himself to this woman as the well of grace. But also, I do have to wonder, did Jesus ever get any water? After all, the man was thirsty, but I guess that wasn't the point, was it? Truly, Jesus could

---

17. John 4:29.
18. John 4:32, 34.
19. John 4:35.

have gotten His own drink, but He wasn't the one whose thirst really needed quenching. His thirst was an invitation for this woman never to thirst again, and her rush to town proves that she truly understood the offer. Her jar of water wasn't the only thing left behind at Jacob's well, but also her sin and shame. She dragged herself to the well that day thirsty; she sprinted away filled.

# CHAPTER TEN

# Couch Surfing

*from Kevan*

After college, my friend Thomas and I rented a house together. He got a job as a youth pastor and taught an online college course while I was a counselor at a drug rehab center and wrote comics on the side. The house belonged to someone in his congregation. It was a two-bedroom, two-bath, with a cozy kitchen and living room in between. Perfect for two bachelors striking out on our own.

"Have you ever heard of couch surfing?" Thomas asked me one day.

It conjured an image in my mind of my roommate in swimming trunks, trying to balance himself dramatically while standing on our hand-me-down sectional. I soon learned that was not the idea. While studying abroad, Thomas used an online network to find hosts he could stay with as he took weekend trips around Europe. People all over were happy to open their homes and let him sleep on their couches for a night or two. He had so many great experiences with it that he wanted to give back and pay it forward.

"If I set it all up, would you mind if we open our home?" he asked.

I was happy to do so, and we were excited to see what kind of adventures might come through our door. In the year we had the house, only one "couch surfer" ended up staying with us. A few months after

Thomas set it all up, we received a request from a man in his midtwenties who was on a pilgrimage. Starting on the Carolina coast and heading west, his plan was to cross the continental United States by himself, on rollerblades, while carrying a giant American flag. The house we rented was right in the middle of North Carolina, in a small town called High Point, perfect for pausing to rest after the first few days of what would be a very long trip.

The day he arrived, freezing rain pelted our windows without remorse. I could be remembering it wrong, but I feel like Thomas just opened our front door, and a tall guy with a long nose rolled right into our living room at full speed, landing exhausted and drenched on the couch. Before words were exchanged, he spent a few awkward minutes removing his coat, bag, flag, and rollerblades. Thomas brought him a glass of water, which he gulped down and nodded gratitude. We sat with him while he caught his breath.

As the conversation began, we learned that he was from Michigan and figured traveling in the South over winter would be better than what he was used to. But while it was maybe better than Michigan, he wasn't far enough south to avoid the cold elements altogether. He took a hot shower while Thomas made dinner, and then we played ATARI before heading out to a local coffee shop to hang out with friends.

When we got back that night, a friend of ours came over who always reminded us of Cory Matthews from *Boy Meets World*. We all sat around the living room, chatting until our guest was ready to crash for some much-deserved sleep. At that point, Thomas went to his room, and "Cory" and I went to mine, where I had two beds set up. He got me ready and into one bed and then stayed the night, sleeping in the other. He was there to turn me over periodically and to just be there in case I needed anything else (you know, like those nights when you have to use the restroom at 2 a.m.).

The next morning, "Cory" left for work just as another guy swung by to get me out of bed and help me with a shower. The weather only got worse as the day went on, turning from sleet to snow. Our couch surfer checked the forecast and asked if he could hang around a couple extra days until it calmed down a bit.

That night, we gathered around the television to watch the 2007 movie *3:10 to Yuma*. I don't remember who stayed over that night to help me, but halfway through the movie, a lanky buddy showed up with his fast-food dinner. Our house was on his way home from work, so he often just stopped in like this. With little more than a quiet "hey," he sat down on the floor beside me and ate while watching with us. Near the end of the movie, he checked the time, got up, and left with an equally subtle, "See ya, guys."

On the third afternoon, friends from the coffee shop came over. "Cory" got me up that morning, and another guy, Steve, stayed the night. We all sat up talking for awhile, stories and laughter traded around the room. As we headed to bed, Steve paused, turned back, and opened my bedroom door out to the living room. When our surfer looked up from the couch, Steve gave him his full name and said, "Look me up on Facebook." They exchanged nods, and he closed the door. "What a cool guy," Steve said with a smirk as if he'd just gotten his favorite actor's autograph.

## A New Concept

By the time I was ready to move out of my parents' house and live "on my own," I had stumbled upon a new phenomenon. A caregiving method virtually unheard of in the disability community. It would be another decade before I had a term for it, but it was what I've come to call *peer-to-peer caregiving*. This means I abandoned the presupposed system of hiring nurses and licensed caregivers, and instead, my friends took care of me, and I took care of them.

The impetus for this, you may recall, came a few years earlier, when my band went on tour, and those guys offered to take care of me. From there, I had roommates in college who helped, and when Thomas and I got our house, some of the same college friends were still in the area and offered to keep helping.

A lot of people—myself included at times—have pushed back on the idea. Why not just hire nurses? There are government means to pay for it, they're professionals, and it separates your social life from your need. Having your friends take care of you gets messy. They're not trained, more emotions are involved, and relationship dynamics are at stake on various fronts. They're volunteering, so there's the reliability factor, as they have their own lives, jobs, and families to consider. They're your friends, so you can't boss them around with the promise of a paycheck. You, "the recipient," have to be more vulnerable and ultimately as selfless as they are in the relationship. The reason they're doing it is because you are friends, so you have to honor that friendship on your end too. In peer-to-peer caregiving, it's not all about you, and isn't it being all about you just . . . easier?

From experiencing both methods of caregiving, I've found that it's *always* messy either way. Professionalism, skill set, reliability, emotions, and relationship dynamics—it's all a house of cards. So, if it's going to be a mess, regardless of whether strangers or friends are helping me, I decided at some point that I'd rather navigate that mess with my friends. And it was those old band members, college friends, housemates, and peers who led me to that conclusion because it intertwined our lives to be a richer community together.

People came to see Fluffy Road-kill play concerts, not because our songs were any good, but because they got to watch and participate in a profound friendship on display. Those of you who have lived on college campuses know the intrinsic camaraderie that happens there. Now add in the brotherhood of intimate caregiving, and that already otherworldly camaraderie skyrockets! It's no wonder we continued after college and saw others step into it with us along the way. This is the Kingdom, isn't it? This is what Jesus was talking about when He told John and the gang, "By this all people will know that you are my disciples, if you have love for one another."[1] There is a beauty and depth to this kind of vulnerability (for both parties) that shapes us into the kind of creation we were always meant to be. The world looks upon it with a curiosity that we welcome. The more, the merrier!

## Revolving Door

This cross-country rollerblading couch surfer from Michigan kept a blog on his journey. He mentioned it in passing while he was with us, so for the next few days after he left, we all kept an eye on his website, to see if and what he would post about us. Sure enough, he soon wrote a short blog post about his stop in High Point. He talked mostly about playing ATARI with us and his skating experience thus far. But right in the middle, he referred to our house as having a revolving door. We all had a good laugh when we read this because there was a moment in his visit when he turned to Thomas and me and asked, "Who actually does live here?"

I'm not saying we all should live in communes with 24/7 open-door policies. I'm married now, and Katie and I enjoy a quiet evening alone together now and then. But the key to what our couch surfer witnessed was not just an open-door policy or college dorm life. He experienced these guys embracing our home out of familiarity and ownership, and both naturally because of their response to my needs.

---

1. John 13:35.

Steve, Landon, Eran, Greg, Preston, Travis, Andrew, Hayden, and even our neighbor Phil all came and went on a regular basis to help with my caregiving, to step into my need, and as a result, our house became a place common to them, a second home.

When we invite people into our need, we invite them into our innermost parts. And we have to realize that while that's terrifying for us, it's just as scary for them. Yet at the same time, the payoff for us both is bountiful in a depth of healing, comfort, rest, adventure, and joy like the world can't even imagine. As we say yes to friends, and they say yes as well, our innermost parts become theirs, and theirs become ours. We are "bearing one another's burdens, and thus fulfilling the Law of Christ."[2] And what does that do but fill a crack in that homesick well in our souls as we glimpse the Kingdom Come?

So, it's no wonder we end up in each other's houses and are drawn to one another when we've had that taste and seen what a life together can look like. It's no wonder these friends are so dear to me, and still, I find more as others look on and say, "I want to be part of that." And it's no wonder we all settle into each other's lives with familiarity and ownership.

---

2. Gal. 6:2, paraphrased.

# CHAPTER ELEVEN

# Dropping Wallets, Opening Doors

*from Kevan*

I was recently rolling along through downtown Fort Wayne. It was cloudy and could start raining any minute. Coming from the bank, I hoped to get into the coffee shop before the impending downpour. Despite what Rupert Holmes sings, nobody actually likes getting caught in the rain, especially people in wheelchairs. Memories of my time at the prison in Arkansas came back to me. So, I was on my way, cruising along and making good time. I crossed the street and deftly mounted the curb. With the coming rain and the time of day, hardly anyone else was out. I had the sidewalks to myself. This was my city, and I was flying through like I owned the place.

Since I was coming from the bank, my wallet was in my hand. And my grip is terrible. Why I didn't have the teller put it in my bag when I was there, I'm not sure. They're nice people and always helpful. It's why I bank there in the first place. But on this odd day, of all days, I'd opted to hold it, and that's rarely a good idea for me to do. With the coffee shop in sight, just one block away now, I hit a crack in the pavement and dropped my wallet on the ground.

I slid to a stop and spun around. There it was . . . just lying there. I turned left and right, looking for someone to help. Gray clouds crept in overhead. I looked down the block. Maybe I could race down and get my barista friend to come help me. But he was working alone that afternoon and couldn't just leave his post. I knew this, and besides, that would mean leaving my wallet on a city sidewalk, out of sight, for three minutes, maybe more. A lot can happen to a wallet in three minutes.

Where was everyone? Fort Wayne is quiet but not a ghost town. We have people here! I promise!

I started to wonder if I needed to stop a car on the road to ask for help. Just before I acted on that bad idea, someone came around the corner. By his gait and tattered clothing, I guessed he was homeless. As he got closer, I was sure of it. He walked with his head down, shoulders forward—not in a sketchy or threatening way, but dejected. He assumed the world didn't see him.

As I watched him walk toward me, I wondered how he would respond to my request. I couldn't get a read on whether he was a necessarily nice person, but he didn't seem like the kind of guy who would steal from me. So, I chose to trust him and waited beside my wallet for him to come by. When he was close, I smiled and nodded a greeting, rolling a little toward him to acknowledge I wanted to say something.

"Hey, sir," I said.

He slowed, not stopping altogether, to listen. The awkwardness of it all was heavy in the air between us. I could tell he was confused that I saw him and nervous that I wanted to talk with him. But he nodded ascent, so I continued.

"I dropped my wallet," I said, betraying embarrassment. "Would you mind picking it up for me?"

His eyes bulged, and his pace picked up again. He shook his head vigorously.

"Nah, nah," he insisted. "I ain't touching that!"

I guessed he didn't believe me that it was mine. I laughed to ease his spirit.

"No," I said lightly. "It really is mine. I promise. I just can't pick it up."

He repeated himself that he wouldn't touch it. As he moved away from me, he said something to reveal his real fear—that I was setting him up, framing him for theft. It caught me off guard. I was dumbfounded. I tried to clarify that that wasn't the case and tried to reason with him, but he was already on his way down to the next block, repeating to himself that he wouldn't touch it.

This was not my first or last interaction with the homeless community. I've had some pretty amazing experiences and would consider many of these guys friends, especially here in Fort Wayne. But never have I been seen as a threat or untrustworthy. Or did this gentleman not feel like I trusted him?

## Trust and Dignity

In studies on emotional attachment between people, there is a principle called "felt safety."[1] You can't *tell* children, for example, that they're safe in a situation. It may be true that they're safe, and you can say it in every way possible, but it won't matter until they *feel* safe to their core. Only then will they experience the brain-chemistry benefits of safety, namely rest and the capacity to heal. I wonder if the same could be said of dignity. We can trust someone and tell them so until we're blue in the face, but until they *feel* trusted, they won't have the capacity to enjoy the freedom of it.

Inviting others into my need is an act of trust. My vulnerability

---

1. Dr. Karyn Purvis, Dr. David Cross, and Wendy L. Sunshine, *The Connected Child: Bring Hope and Healing to Your Adoptive Family* (McGraw Hill, 2007), 48.

is a house, and everyone who enters comes in through the front door. They could tear the place apart, steal my stuff, and eat me out of house and home. But I've chosen to assume they won't, and I let them in as such—a guest that is given a key. It doesn't even come up; that's how much I trust them. I hope this gives them a sense of dignity. I hope they're more whole because of the sense of felt trust at their core that someone has let them in so deeply.

Some struggle with it, but many embrace it and thrive. They feel trusted and rise to the occasion, growing in integrity as a response. A lot of men, especially, respond well to this. It's the change we see when a man becomes a big brother, husband, or father. Responsibility is entrusted to him, and his chest puffs out a bit with it. He walks taller, combs his hair, and pays attention to things he would've missed before.

Need provides us with an opportunity to experience this call into trustworthiness. It could even be argued that need gives us the *only* opportunity to trust and be trusted. When else would trust come into play but when a need is present to be met? See it in the following examples: a big brother steps up because his siblings need leading and protecting, a husband provides for his wife, or a father is the shelter for his children. We have been called to serve, to hold others' lives with care in our hands, and to lay our own lives down for the sake of theirs. When we are presented with these opportunities, we are being invited to live in closer resemblance—and proximity—to the way we were intended to exist all along. That's why something deep inside us stirs, coming to life again out of hibernation, when we feel trusted by our fellow man and when we step into his need.

## My Friend

I have a friend who has schizophrenia. He walks with a strut, the opposite air of Wallet Guy. Chest out, chin high, he swings his arms with a sort of brazen authority. Sometimes, he's the nicest guy in the world and gives bellhops a run for their money. Other times, he'll warn you not to get too close. Either way, you can usually hear him from a few blocks away, his scratchy bark bouncing off the city walls. He is often homeless, and most people make a wide berth of him on the street corners. But we've gotten to know each other over the years, and I look forward to seeing—or hearing—him downtown.

One of my favorite things about this friend is his response when I, or anyone else, ask him for help. I'll need a door opened, a chair moved, a lid taken off a coffee cup. Whatever it is, he is on it in no time! There have been times I've found him lying on the sidewalk, half asleep, but as soon as he sees me coming, he leaps up and runs either to me to give me a hug, or to the door to open it for me. He even kissed me on the cheek once; he was so happy to be of service.

In a world where he has been kicked out of every soup kitchen around, and every cop in town knows his name, my friend can still open doors for people. And in so doing, he can be entrusted with something; he can feel helpful and have a better sense of dignity. In those moments, as he greets me on the sidewalks of Fort Wayne, I get to see joy in his eyes and a different kind of pride in his step. My friend, often homeless, wrought with tattoos, addictions, and a multiple personality disorder, is made human and whole again as he enters into my need.

# CHAPTER TWELVE

# The Spotless Lamb Needed a Wash

*from Tommy*

We are surrounded by dust. The stuff is everywhere, in us and around us. In the time of the New Testament, and most of the world still today, roads were nothing but dust. So, when you arrived at someone's house as a visitor, it was customary to wash up. You brought in a lot of dust with you, namely on your feet. Jesus even washed His disciples' feet at the Last Supper, a sign of servitude and care. But Jesus had dusty feet too. God incarnate needed His feet washed after walking roads and coming in to visit friends.

When He entered the home of a Pharisee named Simon, Luke's gospel account tells us Jesus sat down to eat with His host and company:

> And behold, a woman of the city, who was a sinner, when she learned that he was reclining at a table in the Pharisee's house, brought an alabaster flask of ointment, and standing behind him at his feet, weeping, she began to wet his feet with her tears and

wiped them with the hair of her head and kissed his feet and anointed them with the ointment.[1]

It is tempting to jump right into Jesus' need and His interaction with the woman. But if we start with the gravity of dust, then maybe we can understand the weight of cleansing feet of it.

## Weight of Dust

Jesus is truly God and truly human. And what could be more human than dust? In their latest discovery, evolutionary cosmologists finally have an "answer" to our origin: the carbon from which we are composed is the same as that in stars. "We are stardust!" they proclaim, drowning out their still unanswered question of place or purpose. But anyone who's read the Bible already knows we came from dust: "Then the LORD God formed the man of dust from the ground and breathed into his nostrils the breath of life, and the man became a living creature."[2] There is a profound divide between faith in chance and faith in the Creator. One sees the equation Matter + Time, and the other sees God + Word, yet apparently, both can agree now on one thing: We are all dust.

As fascinating and helpful as modern science can be, we don't need it for wisdom. Solomon was blessed with the curse of being given the most wisdom, wealth, power, and pleasure any man has ever received. At the end of all that, his aged hand penned the sad reality: "What happens to the children of man and what happens to the beasts is the same . . . for all is vanity. All go to one place. All are from the dust, and to dust all return."[3] It may sound dreadfully fatalistic, but that's only because it is, and God said the same thing to Adam and Eve as they left the garden.

---

1. Luke 7:37–38.
2. Gen. 2:7.
3. Eccl. 3:19–20.

We often talk of the "fall of man" from Genesis 3, but from where and to what did man fall? "Cursed is the ground because of you. . . . By the sweat of your face you shall eat bread, till you return to the ground, for out of it you were taken; for you are dust, and to dust you shall return."[4]

Because of the fall, justice demands that flesh return to dust, and to dust our first parents returned—not only our first parents but also all who have come after them. Our inheritance is dust. And it was in that dust that Jesus dirtied His feet upon His humble descent to join us as a man. Dusty feet do not a dirty soul make, but it still had to weigh heavy. Perhaps in this truth, we can understand more about the intimate—yet innocent and holy—connection between our Lord's dusty feet and the woman who washed them.

## Reclining

Jesus once described the Pharisees as "whitewashed tombs,"[5] and the sharp assessment was apt. In a religious culture obsessed with outward cleanliness, the foot was the dirtiest part of one's body that could be near any part of another without sinning. Feet were where the fleshly rubber met the dusty road. The washing of feet was the role of servants in the most affluent homes or the self-imposed job of a truly humble host. And this particular outwardly shiny Pharisee provided Jesus the honor and courtesy of neither.

The feet of Jesus were dusty, an open door for a woman to connect with her Savior. And with her, she brought the only two tools in her possession: a jar of perfume that was perhaps used to call men into sin and her tears, shed perhaps because she shared in those sins with them. Her reasons are not spelled out, but the indignation of a whitewashed tomb and Jesus' reactions—to the woman and His host—are clear to us.

---

4. Gen. 3:17b, 19.
5. Matt. 23:27.

He said to Simon:

"Do you see this woman? I entered your house; you gave me no water for my feet, but she has wet my feet with her tears and wiped them with her hair. You gave me no kiss, but from the time I came in she has not ceased to kiss my feet. You did not anoint my head with oil, but she has anointed my feet with ointment. Therefore, I tell you, her sins, which are many, are forgiven—for she loved much. But he who is forgiven little, loves little."[6]

Jesus did a great many things at this moment, one of which was reshaping decades of mental pathways. That is certainly complex and delicate work, but who better to rewire a brain than the One who knitted it together to begin with? First, if it is the case that this woman lived a life of prostitution, her experience with men, maybe even from childhood, told her there were only two ways to have physical contact with men: either abuse or sex, and often both. And then there was Jesus, who gave her a new idea. Could it be that Jesus was the first man in years, maybe decades, that she had touched in a pure way?

Second, He defended her. Simon and the rest of the tombs were disgusted by the woman, her presence, and her tearful offering to Jesus. The text tells us she was a woman of sin, and we can surmise her presence made quite a scene. But Jesus stood up for her, exalting her as an example of how these whitewashers should have treated Him. Jesus honored her, a woman He culturally shouldn't have been seen with, and defended her against those He culturally should have striven to please. So, this sweet woman at His feet found a new way to interact with men and was also given a new sense of dignity by a man.

It's no wonder the verses that immediately follow this account say,

---

6. Luke 7:44–47.

"Soon afterward, he went on through cities and villages, proclaiming and bringing the good news of the kingdom of God. And the twelve were with him, and also some women who had been healed of evil spirits and infirmities."[7] He treated women differently from the world. He treated them with honor, dignity, and care. True love from the Father. He saw them, lifted them up, defended them, and took delight in their gifts, services, and presence.

Then He said to the woman who'd washed His feet, "Your sins are forgiven."[8] The occasion of filthy feet brought about the restoration, redemption, and worship of a sinful woman. She was the one in need, and Jesus met her need by gifting her the opportunity to meet His. It's a daddy letting his child Band-Aid a scratch and thanking her for treating a ghastly wound. However you feel about the slightly too cute example of a child healing her daddy's boo-boo, the truth of the scene illustrates a reciprocated yet imbalanced humility displayed by Jesus as He allows the tears of a woman to serve the feet of her God. It is a picture of one who is bankrupt, blessing one with infinite wealth, and the bankrupt made wealthy in it.

Jesus served as the lower while reclining as the greater. There was a sense of mystery in Him, maybe even paradox, but never contradiction. Christ, as the servant, wouldn't necessarily just sit back and be served. But He didn't interrupt the woman's work either. He didn't jump to His half-washed feet and insist on washing hers instead, as Peter did later to Him. But just as Jesus did not need to be cleansed of sin, so He did not need to kneel down to wash in this particular situation. He knew what the woman, in her heart, truly needed. And so by accepting honor from the least of these, He became the one honoring her.

---

7. Luke 8:1–2.
8. Luke 7:48.

## Stooping

I wonder if the aroma of the woman's cleansing tears returned to the heart and mind of Jesus in the upper room as He served His disciples in the same manner. "He laid aside His outer garments, and taking a towel, tied it around His waist. Then He poured water into a basin and began to wash the disciples' feet and to wipe them with the towel that was wrapped around Him."[9] Some of the disciples were probably there when the woman served the Lord with her oils and tears. Maybe it came to mind for them now, too, especially at the end, when Jesus instructed them to "go and do likewise."[10]

We read this instruction and know He is telling not just His disciples but us to do it as well. But today's feet wear socks and shoes. The feet of our neighbors will more than likely enter our houses clean. We may even feel some secondhand embarrassment to just imagine our neighbors walking through our doors to that odd moment of shoe removal and toe scrubbing. But perhaps Jesus isn't telling us to wash feet literally. Maybe He is asking us to meet one another's needs with the stooping humility of a foot-washer.

And He doesn't just command His servants without serving first. Jesus gives us, in His own life, these examples of meeting needs by sometimes receiving and sometimes giving, always in humility. The Servant King has both reclined and stooped. He has joyfully received the gift of the poorest in spirit, has given Himself as the most bankrupt, and in both, has showered His children with more riches than even Solomon could dream.

9. John 13:4–5.
10. Luke 10:37, paraphrased.

# CHAPTER THIRTEEN

# The Kingdom of Others

*from Kevan*

D oes looking out for number one ever get old to you? Our culture screams at us that that's what life is all about, but do you ever wonder if there might be something more?

In his second letter to the Corinthian church, Paul talks about our interactions with each other, and more than once—a lot, actually—he says we should be servants to each other and that everything we do should be for the sake of others. He gives us the big picture, too, when he says, "On the day of our Lord Jesus, you will boast of us as we will boast of you."[1] Meaning, in the Kingdom of Heaven, we're going to be praising Jesus and, if we talk about anything else, it won't be ourselves. You'll be raving about me, and I'll be going on and on about you (and even that will all be in the context of praising our Creator)!

The Bible is chock-full of this message that we should serve one another, putting others before ourselves and laying our lives down for each other. Paul writes to the church in Philippi: "In humility count others more significant than yourselves. Let each of you look not only to your own interests, but also to the interests of others. Have this

---

1. 2 Cor. 1:14.

mind among yourselves, which is yours in Christ Jesus."[2] He goes on to say, "Do all things without grumbling or disputing, that you may be blameless and innocent, children of God without blemish in the midst of a crooked and twisted generation."[3] To the Galatians, he writes, "Bear one another's burdens, and so fulfil the law of Christ."[4] And when Paul writes to the Colossian church, he says, "We always thank God, the Father of our Lord Jesus Christ, when we pray for you, since we heard of your faith in Christ Jesus and of the love you have for all the saints, because of the hope laid up for you in heaven."[5]

What I can't find in there is a caveat that I don't need to serve in the case where my need is greater, more obvious, or more time-sensitive than that of my neighbor. He does instruct Titus: "Let our people learn to devote themselves to good works, so as to help cases of urgent need, and not be unfruitful."[6] Even still, I don't see Paul giving those in the urgent cases a pass to "be unfruitful." Yes, some of us do have, in some ways, more demanding, overt, and pressing needs. But everyone is in need, and everyone is called to serve one another. And Christianity is all about honesty, so we're not called to pretend we don't have needs either or sweep them under the rug.

So, what are we supposed to do? I want to listen to my brother as he pours his heart out to me, but I really need help using the restroom before I burst. I see my sister on the verge of tears, but I'm just so hungry right now, cold, cramping, in debt, or lonely. My friend is hurting, but so am I. How do we serve one another despite our own needs? Paul also gives us a glimpse into his own need and God's response to his desire not to have it. He says in 2 Corinthians that the Lord told

---

2. Phil. 2:3b–5.
3. Phil. 2:14–15.
4. Gal. 6:2.
5. Col. 1:3–5a.
6. Titus 3:14.

him, "My power is made perfect in weakness," to which Paul concludes, "I will boast all the more gladly of my weaknesses."[7] What's more, in 1 Corinthians (working backward here), he talks about the resurrection and says, "What is sown is perishable; what is raised is imperishable. It is sown in dishonor; it is raised in glory. It is sown in weakness; it is raised in power. It is sown in the natural body; it is raised in the spiritual body."[8] But the perishable, dishonorable, natural, and (maybe most offensive of all to us) weak can only be raised into something greater if it is sown. Just like a seed is useless if never planted, if we never do anything with ("sow") our weakness, we will never see the power it was meant to bloom into. So, perhaps we're not supposed to serve others *in spite* of our needs but *through* those needs, where God's power is made perfect.

## Some Science for You

Science also speaks to this, according to Dr. David Cross, co-founder and former Rees-Jones Director of The Karyn Pervis Institute for Child Development at Texas Christian University. Dr. Cross is one of the leading experts on studies in childhood trauma and the process of healing through attachment, or as he and Dr. Purvis coined it, Trust-Based Relational Intervention (TBRI). In a discussion with me about the hospitality of need, he pointed out that the "reciprocity of meeting needs is built into our DNA, grounded in our DNA, grounded in our brains."[9]

He said this is because "when mothers are caring for their infants, they get endorphin rushes; the infants get dopamine rushes." We are thought to have four core emotion systems and one of them, Dr. Cross said, "in an infant includes the need to be cared for by an attachment

---

7. 2 Cor. 12:9a.
8. 1 Cor. 15:42–44.
9. Dr. David Cross, phone call with Kevan Chandler, December 14, 2023.

figure *as well as* the attachment figure's need to care for the infant. And in the grownup, it's just a more developed version of that system in the infant." In other words, these chemical responses are in our makeup, not just between mothers and their babies. Fathers also experience it when caring for their children, and the same happens between spouses when serving one another.

This reciprocal kind of care can be found in the DNA of both women and men (in other words, everyone), and it doesn't come and go from us in seasons of life. It's built into each of us for our whole lives, from conception to death. That's how DNA works. But we can mute or rather suppress it with the noises of pride, shame, and selfishness until we forget it's even there. Essentially, we starve or deprive ourselves of a gift God gave us in order to draw us closer to Himself and each other. Instead, we stuff it into a drawer and only pull it out for babies and spouses, and even those rarely these days. We get glimpses and little tastes, but God intended such a fuller, richer experience for us as His children and creations.

Dr. Cross went on to say, "The building blocks of relationships are interactions, and interactions are always these two-way streets." In fact, the first two Pillars of Secure Attachment (a popular theory in psychology that Dr. Cross employs) are to "Give Care" and "Receive Care." These two pillars make up half of the algorithm by which psychologists measure a healthy relationship: Can the parties involved give care and also receive it? If these capacities are present in a relationship, along with the ability to "Negotiate Needs" and "Practice Autonomy," that relationship and the people in it are considered healthy. And that spans mental, spiritual, and physical health because our relationships with others—on both our part and theirs—affect us at all three levels. This makes sense if God really did create need within us as a tool to make us whole. If it's broken, we feel it through and through. But this is why

Jesus came: to fix the break and reconnect us to God and one another. We also get to see Him live out the perfect example of healthy attachment in the Gospels, and not only Paul but apostles John and Peter, as well as the author of Hebrews, all place enormous weight on fellowship and caring for one another as the body of Christ.

## Hospitality

Our need can be hospitable, opening a door to deeper fellowship and healing, a door into true communion. In hospitality (hosting), we say to our guests, "Come in and give me your time, attention, and presence, all for your sake." We assume our space and company will benefit the people we invite. With the idea of need (vulnerability), we say to our guests, "Come in and give me your time, attention, and presence, all for my sake." I wonder if this has to be the case or if the two ideas are not actually as divergent as we've made them out to be. Maybe they overlap. Maybe there can be hospitality in our need too. Maybe inviting others into our vulnerability is an open door into that space Nouwen talks about, where we can find our souls.

We're not talking about asking for help. Let's set that concept aside for now because what we're talking about is deeper than that. One of my favorite authors is my friend S. D. Smith. There's a recurring lesson in many of his books, a question posed by the teacher to his student: What do you have on hand to use as a weapon?[10] Typically, the student will list his sword and maybe his fists early on. Then the teacher will shake his head and list ten other things around him that could've been used: that branch, the bike peddles, his sleeve, his shoe, his opponent's momentum.

What we're talking about is not getting our needs met. We're

10. S. D. Smith and J. C. Smith, *Jack Zulu and the Waylander's Key* (Story Warren Books, 2022), 203–4.

talking about looking at the needs of others and asking ourselves what we have on hand to help them. When asking about this, most of us will list money, strength, or some specific skill to offer. And if we don't have those, we write ourselves off as useless or in greater need than them. I promise I'm not shaking my head at you, but I do challenge you to look again because maybe—just maybe—you'll find something that "you should have listed among our assets in the first place,"[11] namely your own weakness, vulnerability, or need.

This is tricky because we are still, ultimately, talking about *our* need. We are the ones doing the inviting (dare I say it, the asking), and the surface result of the invitation is that our need is still met. There's no getting around that. But from what heart is that invitation coming? Are we putting ourselves first, or others? How do we view our need? How do we view those we are inviting into it? All of this informs how we do the inviting and how we respond to the outcome. It can also give us a foreshadowing of how comfortable or uncomfortable we may feel in the Kingdom of Heaven.

We live in a culture obsessed with self-advocacy and self-care, but those routes are desolate and will leave us empty and alone. I think the picture Paul paints for us in 2 Corinthians is pretty amazing. As believers, a day will come for us when our selfishness will melt away in the presence of Jesus, and our focus will be solely on Him and everyone else. "And the things of earth will grow strangely dim,"[12] including (maybe especially) ourselves. We won't be weighed down anymore by the worries of our own preservations or accolades. We will never again be scared, proud, jealous, annoyed, lustful, or greedy. The last of us will

---

11. *The Princess Bride*, directed by Rob Reiner (1987; Century City, CA: 20th Century Fox, 2000), DVD. Quote is paraphrased.

12. Helen Howarth Lemmel, "Turn Your Eyes Upon Jesus," *Hymnal.net*, https://www.hymnal.net/en/hymn/h/645.

be first, and the first will be last, and we'll weep with laughter to see who exactly that ends up being.

And can I tell you something odd? I don't think we'll miss being selfish at all. I don't even think it will be a word or memory to us in that marvelous city, and if some greasy peddler could sneak in and whisper it into our ears, we'd swat him away like a gnat. That's what Jesus' presence does—it turns our priorities on their heads. He makes us whole so that there is nothing left to advocate for ourselves, and in that wholeness, we are set free to turn our full attention on Him and on others.

Can I tell you one more odd thing? This is the life He has called us to, not just on streets of gold far off in the future, but here and now. It will be made perfect in the end because sin will be out of the way, but we still have the Holy Spirit now, and Jesus said He's with us. So, let's live in the wholeness of His presence, behold His glory, and put others before ourselves. This is where we will find satisfaction, rest, and peace.

# CHAPTER FOURTEEN

# Shaking the World

*from Kevan*

M y friends and I had been in Europe for about a week and a half. Of our own accord, we left my wheelchair home in the States, and these guys carried me in a backpack everywhere we went. A world usually inaccessible became our playground. So far on our trip, we had danced with gypsies, run away from nuns, and gotten ourselves lost in Paris more times than I care to mention. And we still had a mountain in the ocean off the coast of Ireland to climb later. But for now, we were in England, visiting a lovely couple in a small town just south of London. They opened their home to us and let us do what we needed after our busy time in France.

During our stay with them, we rested, listened to records, and took the train into London a few times to wander around. We also went for a couple of hikes in the countryside surrounding their home, which our host was happy to lead. He was a jovial man, full of spunk and curiosity, and a smirk always in tow to warn of his mischief. Being in public with him, you might've wondered if you were the last person on earth he had left to meet and that had just been taken care of.

One of his many friends was a man from Nepal who had come to start a restaurant some years ago. The restaurant went off well, featuring his native cuisine, so he decided to open another, honoring his Italian wife. To make it the best it could be, he hired a staff almost entirely comprised of folks from Italy, and our host (who was in real estate) provided them all with places to live. This, of course, came with some perks, namely free desserts at the restaurant. So one night, we all went out for dinner at Cucina Italia, the fanciest restaurant I had ever been to.

The guys and I were halfway through "backpacking" around Europe, so our semi-clean T-shirts didn't exactly match the standards of the other patrons. Men wore tuxedoes, and women donned diamond necklaces over black dresses. The owner assured us we were fine, but there was still one glaring difference between us and our surroundings. If we weren't vagabond enough already, I was also being carried in a backpack, and this place was clearly an institution of high etiquette. We were throwing off the well-established vibe of the room.

We had a similar experience the next week in Ireland, on that mountain in the ocean. Skellig Michael is a place of rich history, a jagged rock sticking out of the Atlantic with a sixth-century monastery at its peak. The six hundred stone steps leading upward are steep and winding, so that its innate dangers, along with its Christian heritage, make it a walk of reverence for all who set foot there.

I was carried up those old steps about three-quarters of the way by my friend Tom, our friend Luke filming every bit of it. From there, we stopped to rest and take in the view. Then Philip, another friend, carried me the rest of the way up. We reached the top, rounded the monastery, and then headed back down to the same midpoint, where Tom took over again for the rest of the descent.

At the start of our climb, a kindly groundskeeper pulled us aside. He had sprigs of gray hair tucked behind his ears, and they fluttered in the Irish wind as he encouraged us to be careful, to take our time, and to watch our steps. Looking up at the climb ahead of us, we agreed wholeheartedly and did just that.

Tom squeezed the trekking poles as he placed one before the other and then again. Philip held on tight for support to the heavy chains drilled into the rocks. We were often passed by other hikers, slipping around us when the path afforded them space. After all, my guys had a person on their backs, so our pace would be different from that of our fellow pilgrims.

## Rich

At times, it got to me. I wasn't there to intentionally affect anyone else's experience in England or Ireland. Like everyone else, my friends and I just wanted to eat some ravioli and see a monastery. But because our circumstances were different, due to my needs, we stuck out like a sore thumb, caused a ruckus wherever we went, and inevitably got in other people's way.

It's the story of my life and the common narrative of need. Whether I'm traveling or at home, because of my disability, pretty much anything I do is going to require more of me and others. I don't like this fact for myself or my friends and family. Everything takes longer. Everything takes more forethought and effort. Everything involves more people and also disrupts more people. There's a temptation to assume this is a bad thing, but maybe it's actually a grace.

One of my favorite songwriters, Rich Mullins, once wrote, "From the place where morning gathers, you can look sometimes forever 'til you see what time may never know . . . how the Lord takes by its corners this old world, and shakes us forward and shakes us free."[1] I wonder if need is one of the ways the Lord takes by its corners this old

---

1. Rich Mullins, "Calling Out Your Name," track 6 on *The World as I Remember It*, vol. 1, Reunion Records, 1992, compact disc.

world. Perhaps our inconveniences are more liberating than we often give them credit for.

Needs shake us, whether they belong to us or someone else. If we're in proximity, they can change us. They can cause us—force us—to slow down or keep up, to think and act differently from our norm. They can pull us out of our comfort zones and disrupt the ideal rhythms by which we usually function. They can either set right the broken or break the too-perfect.

Concerning "troubles" and "interruptions," C. S. Lewis once pointed out to his friend Owen Barfield at the start of World War II that "since nothing but these forcible shakings will cure us of our worldliness, we have at bottom reason to be thankful for them."[2] He even goes as far as to call these shakings God's "surgical treatment." Rich seemed to have the same idea as he wrote his song.

Our Father loves us dearly and calls us back to Himself, and often utilizes the inherent needs He designed us with—broken though they are now by sin—to show us the way home. Needs can shake us forward and shake us free, to delve deeper into vulnerability and fellowship: the next line of Rich's song calls it hope. What we find there, if we go, is a sense of holy purpose and belonging, unlike anything the rest of the world can offer. We find the attachment God created us to experience with Him, His Trinity, and each other.

## Ravioli

As we bumbled to our table at Cucina Italia, my backpack, carried by a friend of mine with particularly wide shoulders, bumped chair backs and tuxedoed shoulders in the narrow aisles. To seat our crew, waiters shifted tables together nervously and then stared at us, unsure

---

2. Clive Staples Lewis, *The Collected Letters of C.S. Lewis, Volume II: Books, Broadcasts, and the War, 1931-1949* (HarperCollins, 2004), 232.

how to set up the chairs with me in mind. The other tables around us stopped eating to watch, curious how this odd scene would play out.

At this point, we would usually lower my backpack to the floor, take me out and sit me back into it sideways, then put two chairs together, facing each other for a broader surface, and lift me up—in the backpack—to sit atop the two chairs. This way, I could be at about eye level with everyone else at the table. It had been our host's idea a few days earlier, and we'd adopted it for most meals. That night, though, considering the whole process with the world watching, I was ready to give up, head back to the house, and order a pizza. But that's not what Tom had in mind. Neither did Philip, Ben, or the couple we were staying with.

Without a second thought, Philip and Ben started moving chairs. Tom helped our wide-shouldered friend pull me off his back and lower me to the ground, a long way down, considering his tree-like height. Philip and Ben moved plates and glasses to fit our new arrangement, while our hosts chatted with the waiter to ease his worries. Ben, a lanky torpedo, scooped me out of the backpack and turned me around to sit sideways in it. In the trapeze act, my feet only barely missed a man's head at the table behind us.

Just then, the voice of a lady chimed from nearby.

"Do you need any help?" our victim's wife asked.

"Sure," Ben said unashamedly.

Immediately, the man we almost kicked hopped up to help, along with three others. To make room for the turned chairs—my "throne"—they shifted our row of tables a bit more and even adjusted their own chairs. As they helped, smiles broke out across the men's faces, and laughter came tumbling out too. When was the last time they'd broken a sweat like this, and alongside their fellow man?

A lightheartedness fell over the room. Having met the owner the night before in a more casual setting, I can't help but wonder if this sight brought him joy. He was, after all, a man full of smiles and aimed to fill others with light. The team got me all set up, and the men returned to their wives and dinners a little different from when they had first sat down that evening.

## Boats

As we came down the side of Skellig Michael, I could feel Tom's labored breathing. It had been a long day, with a seven-mile boat ride and a strenuous climb up the island. He was exhausted, and so was Philip. I was, too, for that matter. We were ready to be back on the mainland with the rest of our team, enjoying fish and chips at a pub. Just a few hundred steps left to go, and then the boat ride back.

Far below, we could see our boat waiting, the captain growing impatient. We were going as fast as we could, but that wasn't very fast, and downhill requires more caution than up, so tensions mounted. And the queue at our heels was piling up. My head pounded with the words of our captain when we were getting off the boat two hours earlier. He'd said if we weren't back in time, he'd leave us. I believed him. No one dared to go around us because of where we were on the path and the need for safety upon descent. And that meant their captains were waiting for them too.

I was getting self-conscious again, the whole island lining up behind us, everyone running late to their boats. But Tom carried on. He squeezed the trekking poles and took another step down. Philip stayed close, spotting us as we slowly went. When a step was wider, or Tom just felt confident, he would pause for a moment of rest. Taking advantage of the beat, he would look up and out across the water, taking in the view with a smile.

"Wow," he'd say, and sometimes he'd just laugh and shake his head.

Philip got distracted by rocks or the occasional puffin popping out to watch us. Even in the rush of getting back to the boats and home, my friends still found joy in our journey. And I couldn't help but do the same. The guys and I had to go slowly, which offered us the profound opportunity to truly see the world around us. We could have pushed through, stressing about the time and what others would think or say of us. Instead, we accepted the hospitality of need and enjoyed the sweet moment we found ourselves in.

Two hours earlier, we had looked up at an impossible climb, and now we made our descent from the top. We stood on an island with a 1,500-year-old monastery on it, not somewhere you get to be every day. The epic experience was coming to an end, and because of our need to rest and step carefully, that end was delayed a bit . . . not just for my friends and me.

About halfway down the mountain, when the line behind us was at its longest, people began talking to us. At first, a few of them just kindly said, "No problem," when we looked back to apologize. After awhile, their "No problem" turned into "Take your time." Then, encouragement, and finally, conversation. The pile-up became a parade of heroes. We descended all together, laughing and talking, reveling in life, relishing the vast wonder of creation, enriched by the camaraderie around us.

And no one missed their boats.

# CHAPTER FIFTEEN

# The Way Needed a Ride

*from Tommy*

When Jesus reached Jerusalem at the beginning of His last week on earth, He told His disciples to find a donkey for Him to ride. This would mark His entrance, like a king coming into town after a battle—but instead of a mighty steed, Jesus requested a donkey. In Mark's account, Jesus gave them specific instructions:

> "Go into the village in front of you, and immediately as you enter it you will find a colt tied, on which no one has ever sat. Untie it and bring it. If anyone says to you, 'Why are you doing this?' say, 'The Lord has need of it and will send it back here immediately.'"[1]

The Lord had need of it. The Creator of the universe needed a colt, but it couldn't just be your run-of-the-mill used colt with a new coat of wax to bring out the shine. It had to be fresh, right off the showroom floor, and never been ridden. What a bizarrely precise need. Why? Matthew gives some insight in his account when he says it took place to fulfill Zechariah's prophecy: "Say to the daughter of Zion,

---

1.  Mark 11:2–3.

'Behold, your king is coming to you, humble, and mounted on a donkey, on a colt, the foal of a beast of burden.'"[2]

It fulfilled prophecy. Good to know. But what are the prophetic rhymes and reasons for God's ordinance? A prophet foresees things that God has willed, and God ordains everything on purpose, for a purpose. Nothing rogue, nothing random. Jesus is the Alpha and Omega, the bookends of all existence, and He is not higgledy-piggledy about what is placed on the shelf.

## Prophecy

So, why did the Lord, the God of everything, ordain this colt ride in the first place? Why would Jesus need to need, of all things, a donkey? If the answer starts and ends with "to fulfill prophecy," we make a nice tidy loop for ourselves, but a nice tidy loop is also the accurate description of a snare. God doesn't bury an acorn in the dead of night so that He can proclaim "TREE!" in the morning. He doesn't practice circular sovereignty to prove His supremacy, so we don't need circular doctrine to prove His existence or goodness.

Back to our question at hand. "Why?" The prophet only foresees what God has ordained, but why did God ordain a donkey? The answer is not so far off from the reason why He needed a womb.

Jesus came down from a throne. He will come again on a warhorse.[3] And these old tokens of kingship are easy for us to grasp. Kings are high and mighty. So is God. But He stooped below the face of heaven to form Adam in the dirt and walked with him in the garden. God walked with Abraham, Jonathan,[4] the disciples, and the woman at the well. And He walks with us still to this day. He heals people, forgives

---

2. Matt. 21:4–5.
3. Rev. 19:11.
4. 1 Sam. 14:45.

sin to resurrect the sinner, washes our feet, and seats us with Him. He told His disciples, "I'm going away to build a house for you."[5] Jesus is a king, on high and almighty, but this same King is a humble servant, gardener, carpenter, and shepherd who gave His life for the whole flock of His oh-so-prone-to-wander sheep. He brings, as Zechariah also says, salvation.[6]

If we could zoom out from it all and see Jesus as the Alpha and Omega, we would see Him as the King we worship, whose righteousness is beyond eternal, overflowing into infinity, holding everything as the bookends of creation. But this day in Jerusalem, He was seated on a donkey in the middle of those bookends.

For Israel then and all followers of Jesus now, we long for our ruling King to come; we are ready for His reign. But there's a lot more to God than judgment, vengeance, and royalty. He needed a colt because that's what the humble rode on. It's what His mom rode when she was carrying Him in her womb. Paul writes to the Philippians:

> Christ Jesus, who, though he was in the form of God, did not count equality with God a thing to be grasped, but emptied himself, by taking the form of a servant, being born in the likeness of men. And being found in human form, he humbled himself by becoming obedient to the point of death, even death on a cross.[7]

And whether anyone connected the dots that day to the prophecy, He told the crowd by His choice of ride precisely who He was and what He was there to do without ever conceding in the slightest His role as King of Kings. In fact, His entrance only served to further demonstrate the role and His eternal sovereignty over it.

---

5. John 14:2, paraphrased.
6. Luke 1:68–79.
7. Phil. 2:6–8.

## Prince of Peace

For a few moments, Jerusalem thought they were welcoming their long-promised liberator and conquering King, a crown and sword in hand. Palm branches and cloaks flew out! Shouts of "Hosanna" rang in the streets! You'll notice they weren't even taken aback by the donkey. In that time, kings actually rode donkeys on occasion, which was traditionally in peacetime. It was a way of saying to his people, "I've put away my warhorse for now because he's not needed; this old clunker of a donkey will do just fine." But the celebrating Jews were under Roman occupation, and little did they (or the disciples) know that Jesus was about to be crucified. This was, for everyone involved, anything but peacetime.

Maybe they saw it as a foretaste that Jesus was preemptively trading in His warhorse for the soon-to-be-needed donkey. Maybe they just figured it was all He could get in a pinch. Maybe they were blinded by the hype and missed altogether that it was a donkey amid the crowds and showers of wild praise. But one thing is certain: Jesus chose a donkey and rode it into the City of David because He was and is and forever will be the Prince of Peace. By this kind of ride, Jesus was preparing a table in the presence of His enemies and inviting to come and sit "all you who are weary."[8] His donkey was, in a sense, an invitation for the hurting world to rest, and asking His disciples to fetch the colt for Him was His invitation for them to participate in setting the table. He wasn't promising a victory to come; He was victory Himself, present and accounted for with peace in tow.

Jesus did ride in as a conqueror, but conquerors are usually demanding tyrants, and this God only demands our greatest joy, peace, and wholeness. The greatest satisfaction an image bearer can find is

---

8.  Matt. 11:28 NIV.

when he is abiding in the glory of the One whose image he bears. In Jesus' immutable nature, we find humility and grace: the kind of humility that chooses to ride on a beast of burden instead of a gleaming white stallion and the kind of grace that ushers into the middle of a nightmare peace that passes all understanding.

Once again, Jesus humbled Himself, stooping as He always had, from the forming of Adam all the way to the cross. He needed to ride something because He was the glorious king, and He needed to ride a colt because He was the peaceful servant—everything on purpose, for a purpose. If Jesus had ridden in on a horse that day, it would have been a grand scene, but His crucifixion at the end of the week wouldn't have made sense. Instead, He stooped and stooped and stooped lower still to get closer to you and me, bringing with Him salvation and peace. Hosanna in the highest!

# CHAPTER SIXTEEN

# Alive . . . and a Choice Not to Be

*from Kevan*

### Bad Idea #1

A year after going to Europe, I was invited to share about my experience at a church in Southern California. Some of the friends who went with me to Europe came along as well. Luke, Ben, and Tom each had specific roles on our intercontinental adventure. Everyone did a bit of everything, but specialties fell in as such: Luke was the filmmaker, Ben was the caregiver, and Tom was the instigator.

These roles took shape by each personality mixing with team dynamics. They carried over naturally from that trip to this one. And, if you've ever seen photos or videos of me being carried in precarious situations, I am more than likely on Tom's back, which is where I once again found myself.

We visited the church a day early, to meet the staff and scope out the setup. I had my wheelchair and rolled around the stage, getting my bearings. The guys, all three being musicians, snooped around the drum set and guitar rigs. My cousin, Kyle, worked at the church, so he gave us the five-cent tour, which ended in the green room. He betrayed a goofy grin.

"You guys wanna go up in the rafters?" he asked, glancing around in case his bosses might overhear.

I liked the sound of that, and so did the others. Ben ran to the car to get our backpack, and I was soon on Tom's back, ready to go. Kyle led us down one hallway, then another, and another. They didn't make the access easy to find, and I soon understood why. Eventually, we came to a ladder leading upward into a dark hole in the ceiling. Kyle leaned casually on the ladder and pointed up.

"Well," he said cheekily. "Up you go."

Tom took hold of the first rung, and that's when my opinion changed. I realized I'd never climbed a ladder before, let alone one that would take us eighty-some feet off the ground. Suddenly, I didn't think this was such a great idea.

"Tom," I said.

"Kevan," he mimicked.

I had a quick decision to make. If I said no—which part of me really wanted to—I would be back in my chair in no time, safe and sound on solid ground while my team went on without me. If I said yes—well, I didn't know what would happen then. But I'd spent three weeks in Europe with these guys and known them for several years before that. They had always taken great care of me, aside from the occasional bumped head, scratched-up tailbone, and a broken nose.

I was torn, but I had a choice to make, and I chose courage in light of my friends' character. They loved me and really did look out for me, through any obstacle. And we'd had some scrapes, but it was always worth it, and we were still alive to tell the tales.

So, I said yes, and we made the ascent.

If you've ever been in a large venue and looked up, where all the can lights and catwalks hang in what feels like outer space, that's what we stepped out onto. House lights at our elbows lit the ground as we moved along narrow walkways, crouched and barely fitting. We looked down on the massive stage we had just been standing on a few minutes earlier, and it seemed so small now. A technician came out onstage to check some mic cables, and it was funny to realize he had no idea we were up there, just overhead. The world stood still for a moment as we hung suspended above it.

I was glad I had said yes.

## Bad Idea #2

When the speaking engagement was done, we had a few days off before heading home. One of those days, we took a walk together on the beach. Sand doesn't go well with wheelchairs, so I was once more in the backpack on Tom's back. As we strolled along the shoreline, he spoke over his shoulder to me.

"Kevan," he said with confidence. "As your friend and the one carrying you here and now, I feel like it's my God-given duty to get you into the water."

I was faced again with a choice.

"Okay," I said. "Not too far, though."

"We'll start small," he assured me.

We waded out until he was just over his knees. Waves rolled up to meet his waist, getting my bare feet wet; it was refreshing on the hot day. We stood there for a minute, taking it in. Then he spoke over his shoulder again to me.

"How are you feeling?" he asked.

"Good," I said.

What I meant by "good" was that I was happy with our experience as it was. I felt satisfied and accomplished. What Tom heard was that I was ready to go further in. So, without double-checking, he moved forward, past his waist, halfway up his torso. As he got almost chest-deep,

I cried out, trying to sound as calm as I could.

"That's good," I called. "That's good!"

Somehow, he heard me over the roar of the waves, now much bigger. They crashed against his chest, and close to mine, as he stopped walking and planted his feet firmly on the unseen floor of sand. The ocean spray cooled our faces with every watery barrage.

Where we sighed contentedly before in the shallows, we now laughed in the deeps with joy at the miracle of a thrill. A violent, deafening, blue world burst around us like watery fireworks, and we held our own. We were just a couple of little human pillars braving one of the mightiest wraths creation could muster, and we loved it.

After a few minutes and a few close calls of losing our balance, we returned to dry land, now truly satisfied and accomplished. A para surfer who had been moving across the horizon not far from us came into land as well. He seemed in a hurry, abandoning his board and letting the wind carry him in. As we reunited with Luke and Ben, the flustered surfer ran up to us.

"Did you not see?" he asked in broken English. "There was a shark."

He went on to explain that right after we left it, he had crossed over the spot where we'd been standing in the tide and was met there by a circling shark. In the beginning, God created everything and instructed man to "fill the earth and subdue it."[1] That day on the beach, Tom and I stood in a place we shouldn't have been able to get to, against elements infinitely bigger and stronger than us, encircled by a creature we shouldn't have survived being around; and we found—on all accounts—that we could.

---

1. Gen. 1:28.

## Bad Idea #3

At the end of our California visit, the guys and I went for a hike along Runyon Canyon, overlooking Los Angeles. The sun was slowly setting, painting the sky in layers of orange across the day's light blue. Ben and Tom took turns carrying me. We followed the trail with a hundred other people who were out for their evening walks. Some talked on cellphones or with a friend beside them, others listened to music with earbuds, and some just enjoyed the quiet after a long day at the office.

The first section of the trail was easy. I could have used my wheelchair and had before. But we wanted to go farther this time, so we employed the backpack. A smooth, wide, sandy path got narrower after a while. Dips and bumps began to show up around increasingly winding curves of deeper, looser sand until rocks and steps appeared. We continued the walk, scaling rickety stairs, crossing ravines on worn plank bridges, and finding purchase on desert boulders as we made our way from one to another. All the while, the sun sank to our right and the city lights below flickered to life.

It had been a busy week, and coming to the end of it, I was getting tired. But the view was breathtaking and I was with my friends. Besides, I had no idea when I would be back here with the tools and people needed to experience this part of the trail. My exhausted body absorbed the rocking and bouncing of all-terrain hiking while my mind drifted over the past week and the present growing evening. With every new stairway and bridge we came to, something in me harrumphed. I was ready to head back, to get some rest, and then go home, but I pushed through and "tagged along" with a smile. But with every step, I felt my endurance and attitude slipping.

Finally, we reached a pinnacle on the trail. The path opened onto a landing at the canyon's rim, and on the edge of that landing, a jagged rock stretched out like an arm over open air. We paused for a moment, catching our breath, looking up at the climb out onto the rock. People went ahead of us. We watched as they crawled on all fours up the crude naturally hewn steps in the rock face, then disappeared over the top.

I was on Tom's back.

"Kevan," he said. "How are you feeling about this?"

"I'm gonna wait here," I answered shortly.

"You sure?"

"Yeah. You guys go ahead."

He nodded. The team lifted me off his back and lowered me to the dusty ground. They set me to the side of the path on the landing, out of foot traffic, and faced me toward the sunset. Then all three of them were gone, on all fours, up and over the rock.

Ben came back a few minutes later and sat on the ground with me. We took in the view from there, sitting quietly, but I was disappointed in myself. I had said yes to so much, growing with every new and rich experience my friends and I had together, only to squander it here on a bad mood. Maybe it was legitimately too dangerous, but so are rafters, and so are sharks. And no one looked down on me for the call I made to stay behind on the trail. I was physically tired, to be fair, but my heart was the real issue.

Instead of allowing my need to enhance our lives and fellowship, I used it as an opportunity to forfeit. As a result, I missed out not just on a sight, but on an experience shared with my friends and fellow man. I had no idea what the view was from over that rock, but I knew the view from where I had decided to stop: the feet and knees of everyone else passing me to go further up.

## Alive

In their book *Safe People*, Dr. Henry Cloud and Dr. John Townsend say, "You aren't alive if you aren't in need."[2]

My life has been stacked with experiences that I still can't believe I've gotten to be part of. High adventure in the world and profound depth in the heart, none of which I've done on my own. Because of my physical needs, I've rarely been alone. It's worked out well that I'm an extrovert and prefer being around people because they have accompanied me in practically everything I do. And this company I've kept has led to the wonderful experiences I've had.

It's not just people saying yes to my need, but me saying yes to their participation. Ultimately, we are *both* walking through the door that need opens for us. It's a door into beautiful fellowship, a life together like we were created to have, full of intimacy, grace, and shared strength. It's where we find that high adventure and profound depth alongside others who are carried by us or carry us. But we have to respond to need's hospitality. We have to say yes. We have to go through the door. Otherwise, are we really alive?

---

2. Cloud and Townsend, *Safe People*, 131.

# CHAPTER SEVENTEEN

# On the Floor

*from Kevan*

B y the end of our trip to Europe with the backpack, my friends and I had come to recognize two things: a lot of people were paying attention to us, and they didn't need an explanation beyond what they saw to know what was going on. Our little group of travelers was a spectacle, bashing around Europe with one of us in a backpack. Anyone who saw that—up close, across the street, in a crowd, on a train, in the middle of a field—could figure out there was something wrong with me, and these people helping me experience life to the fullest were doing so simply because we were friends. In short, we unintentionally put on display a unique and beautiful kind of brotherly love.

With this understanding, we decided that our next adventure should be somewhere entirely outside our familiar Western culture and the English language. Where could we go to intentionally be a spectacle, relying solely on the visual to be enough? We considered several countries, but it didn't take long to settle on China. The Lord gave us some amazing connections to make it happen, and in September 2018, we were on a plane from Vancouver to Shanghai.

We fished for our dinner in a rural neighborhood pond, squeezed down the narrow alleyways of an old city street market, and walked part of the Great Wall. The people we met were wonderful, and every experience was remarkable. While this trip was profound for me from start to finish, one place in particular has stayed with me more than any other.

## Kiddos on a Hill

Atop a hill on the outskirts of Luoyang sits a big, sky-blue building with clouds painted all over it. A care center run by New Hope Foundation. Standing on the roof, at seven stories tall, you can get a good view of the city and mountain range beyond. The top floors are private quarters for the foreign workers living there and where we stayed when we visited for a week in the middle of our trip. The lower floors house nurseries and playrooms for children, the predominant lodgers of this place.

New Hope Foundation is a nonprofit committed to serving orphans with special needs, particularly in China. They've been around for over twenty years and seen countless little ones come through their doors and arms. At the time, they had close to ninety in their care at the facility we visited.

We arrived late in the evening after all the children were in bed. We ate dinner with the staff and settled into our room. The next morning, after breakfast, the boss, Nate, gave us a tour. He started us on the roof, and we worked our way down until the tour ended in the lobby, where we were greeted the night before. As Nate wrapped up his presentation, a sweet grin crept over his scruffy face.

"Now what?" we all asked, looking at each other.

"Now," he said simply, "we play with the kiddos."

His eyes flashed with joy. He could barely hold back a chuckle. This was his favorite part of the job, ushering people into being present.

"Folks come here from all over the world," he had told me at breakfast. "And they come to work, to fix things, and to do when they really just need to be."

He went on to explain that these children didn't need a new shelf or a light fixture replaced. They needed you to hold their hand, look them in the eye, sing with them, laugh with them, and play with them. They needed you to be present, to "waste time" with them because they needed to know they matter that much.

Nate gestured for us to pick a room.

All the blood rushed to my head. For over thirty years at that point, I had been inviting people into my physical need to feed and play with me and get on my level. Now, I was invited into the needs of others and to get on their level. But I didn't know how to do what was being suggested. Like a robot who could suddenly "not compute," I short-circuited. I froze, wanting to shrink away and disappear. The guy who was usually up for anything was stuck in a doorway to the unknown.

The double-edged sword of being carried around in a backpack, though, is that you go wherever the person carrying you goes. And in this case, the person carrying me was going through the doorway of a playroom, which meant I was too.

The room was green. Thick mats lay across the floor, which turned out to be the case in all the rooms. We removed our shoes and washed our hands. The guys set my backpack, me still in it, down on a mat. Then, one by one, they spread out to each play with a different kiddo.

I watched.

My backpack was situated in the middle of the room, in the heart of the action. One boy, held up by a standing board, had the time of his life, dropping a toy when it was handed to him. His nanny or one of the guys picked it up and gave it back to him, only for him to drop it again with a giggle. It made everyone laugh. A staff member held a precious girl in the corner, singing to her, while another child waddled around the room, checking us all out.

That was the first room. After awhile, we moved on to another. This one was pink. Again, my backpack was placed on the floor, and the guys went off in various directions to play with the kids. One of the workers, Katie, came and sat on the floor in front of me. A little princess came with her, cradled in her arms. That night, I wrote in my journal, "She was only okay with me because of Katie's presence." I don't know if that was true (Katie would argue it wasn't), but it was how I felt about myself.

I couldn't hold these children or crawl or roll on the floor with them. I couldn't pick up toys when they dropped them, couldn't chase them or dance with them. The kiddos who could run around were more interested in the guys who could keep up with them, and the ones on the floor needed someone to pick them up or kneel beside them. Over the years, I had served in prisons and drug rehabs and was even a youth pastor for a bit. But all my ministry experience had been built, unintentionally, on the assumption that the person I served, with a spiritual need, could bring the physical strength to our interaction. We were here with these children to play, and I didn't know how to do that with my limitations bumping up against theirs. How does a body that doesn't work serve another body that doesn't work?

## Our Gifts

In his letter to the exiles, Peter talks about loving one another. He says we do this through hospitality and it's paramount to do because "love covers a multitude of sins."[1] Think about that. The way we love people can set them (and us) free and can turn lives upside

---

1. 1 Peter 4:8.

down. This is powerful stuff, and it rests on how we interact with each other. Peter says, "As each has received a gift, use it to serve one another."[2]

God has implanted in each of us a unique gift, a capacity to love in part the way He infinitely loves us. Mine isn't the same as yours, and yours doesn't look like that of the person next to you. We are fearfully and wonderfully made in God's image, and He is so very immense that there's plenty of room for variety in how His image—His character—manifests in us.

Peter spans a wide swath of gifts with just two examples: words and action. He says of the first, "If you open your mouth, speak the heart of God."[3] Use the words God gives you, not your own. And to the second, the one who serves with his hands, he says to do so "by the strength that God supplies."[4] The strength God gives you. No more, no less, but perfectly measured for you to do what He has called you to do: love whoever's in front of you, like these kiddos in front of me, and me in front of them.

## Toby

The third room was yellow, and it started off the same as the other two rooms. Me in the backpack. Observing.

Until one little boy caught my eye.

Toby lay on his right side on a mat. He was scrawny. His thin limbs stuck out of his shorts and T-shirt, and one of his arms was in a splint, sprawled out heavy and thick in front of him. I wondered if the reason for the splint could be found in his other arm, which was bent up to his mouth. He sucked on his fingers, noisily and without

---

2.  1 Peter 4:10.
3.  1 Peter 4:11, paraphrased.
4.  1 Peter 4:11.

ceasing, his ant-hill chin bobbing up and down. His eyes were soft but aware, taking in the room and newcomers.

I called my friend Ben over.

"Could you lay me on the floor?"

He was happy to do it. He scooped me out of my backpack and laid me on my left side on the mat. I was face-to-face with Toby, who continued to suck on his fingers. But now his eyes were on me, big, brown discs staring into me like I was a whole world to him.

"Hi," I said. "Hey, buddy."

He went on sucking, staring.

"How do those fingers taste?"

Finally, I used my wrist and knuckles to inchworm my left hand closer to him. With the position I was lying in, my hand was the only part of my body I could move. It took everything in me to make the journey a few inches, maybe centimeters, to meet his shoulder. By the time I got there, I was out of breath.

"Hey," I said, feeling silly.

I stretched out my fingers and rubbed his needle-nose shoulder.

"You doin' alright?"

My words felt feeble and trite, so I gave up on them. Instead, we stared at each other for a long time. I rubbed his shoulder between my index and thumb (my only working fingers, but just the right size for the purpose). He sucked away on his fingers. It was so noisy. What if I made the sound too? I pulled my cheeks into my teeth and mimicked the sounds. His gaze grew deeper, acknowledging the language. I did it again, as if in reply to his sounds, and then his seemed to become a response to mine.

We went back and forth in conversation, understanding one another far beyond words. I smiled at my new friend as we fell into fellowship, his eyes enveloping me like a muddy ocean. A new sense of belonging overcame me. In a foreign country, on the floor of an orphanage with a nonverbal, nonmobile child, I was whole. This little boy was seen, and so was I.

Looking back, I can't help but wonder if Toby had the same questions I had that day on how to connect with such limitations. Maybe he had already worked through all that by then, content and secure in the Lord, or maybe this was an affirmation for him. My needs had brought me to this place, and his had brought him. In which case, maybe our needs weren't limitations at all, but the hand itself of God—the strength of God—bringing us each to this moment of truth and beauty. We were both born into challenges that many (in the medical and political arenas, especially) would look upon and deem "incompatible with life." But it's because of those very challenges, terrible as they were and continue to be for us, that we ended up here, to experience communion as the Author of Life joined us, lying on that mat with us and speaking our language.

The room faded away—all the other children, the staff, nannies, and my friends—and Toby, in turn, became a whole world to me. And the world we found ourselves in together was one without end. As the Kingdom of Heaven came down, two broken bodies served one another with the gift of presence, and that gift "by the strength that God supplied."[5] The strength God gave us. No more, no less. Perfectly measured for what He'd called us to do.

5. 1 Peter 4:11, paraphrased.

# CHAPTER EIGHTEEN

# Countless Wingmen

*from Kevan*

atie turned out to be not just "one of the workers." During our week-long stay at the care center in China, this beam of light acted as host to me and the guys. Originally from Illinois, she had moved to the care center to support the nannies, nurses, and staff in finding the best ways to care for these children. But that week, she was in charge of helping our crew navigate a foreign country and keep us out of too much trouble, which ultimately meant we spent a lot of time together.

We explored the city market, walked around the birthplace of kung fu, danced in the park, and played with the kiddos in the center's care. Through it all, I couldn't help noticing how genuinely Katie delighted in everyone she came across—children, staff, visitors like us, and strangers on the street. Whoever it was, they were the whole world to her as she interacted with them, and they left her presence feeling a hundred feet tall.

I had never met anyone like this woman, and I said as much to Ben as we drove off at the end of our visit. On my return to the States, our friendship continued as we stayed in touch. The occasional FaceTime call and a text message here and there grew more frequent in the weeks and months to follow. Katie and I met in the fall of 2018, and by the spring of 2019, I couldn't stop thinking about her! As it turned out, she was feeling the same way. But I was in a wheelchair, and while that didn't bother her, she was concerned whether she could physically take care of me like she'd seen the guys do. And on my end, she was in China doing amazing work. How could I take her away from that? So, without ever talking about it, we both just figured we couldn't be anything more than friends until a mutual friend addressed the obvious.

"Would it be okay if I mention you to Kevan?" she asked, and Katie said yes. Then that friend came to me and said, "I think you should ask Katie out." And whatever reservations I was still holding on to at that point snapped. It was like a dam burst in me; my love for Katie and my desire to be with her finally poured out of my heart by the gallons. This friend later told us that she'd spent time with each of us, and all we talked about was each other. "It was like seeing the most beautiful sunrise. How could I not point it out?"

## First Date

In the summer of 2019, I texted Katie: "Next time we're in the same country, can I take you out to dinner?" She replied with an emphatic, "I would very much like that." I quickly decided I couldn't wait until she was back in the States to make it happen. She had to leave China every two months for her visa to reset, so we met in Australia that September. And this is where a story for the ages puts on display not only the love between a man and woman but a man and his brothers as well—my countless wingmen.

My dad came with me to Australia. My friend Luke joined us as well. He had come to Europe and China as our filmmaker to capture the experiences. This time, Luke was traveling with me on the other side of the lens, to take care of me and to keep everything pure and above reproach for my first-ever date. While my dad did some sightseeing and Luke practiced his architectural photography, Katie and I spent four days exploring downtown Sydney together. We took buses and trains all over (focused more so on the joy of sitting with each other than where we were actually going), shared fish and chips on the beach, and did Tim Tam Slams every evening after dinner.

My dad and Luke didn't just get me ready for bed and turn me at night; they gave me showers and got me ready for the day. They were never too far away throughout the day in case I needed anything. One night, Katie and I were walking through a cathedral courtyard when we happened upon Luke and his camera. Before we parted ways, he helped me with the restroom, just so I would be good to go for awhile.

Luke was one of many guys who helped make the love story of Katie and me possible over the next year. My roommates and the various guys who would stay over at night to take care of me were patient as Katie and I navigated FaceTime calls with a twelve-hour difference across the world. When she came home to visit for Christmas, another friend and his wife traveled with me to Illinois to meet Katie's family and ask her parents for permission to marry her. The "China Crew" (all the guys who went on that trip in 2018) even conspired with me to go to China a second time and surprise her at the care center in February 2020 to propose. But unavoidable COVID-19 protocols brought her to me in the States instead, where I proposed to her in the sunroom of my parents' home, just days before the world shut down.

## Road Trips and Wedding Bells

Even then, one of my good friends offered for me to live with him and his family during that early season of mandatory quarantine. He would single-handedly provide all my caregiving so we wouldn't have guys coming and going to my house in such uncertain times. I appreciated the care, but Katie had just moved to Fort Wayne and was living near my neighborhood. How would I see her if I moved in with this friend's family on the other side of town during quarantine? "We thought of that," he said without missing a beat. "We have a room for her too."

After quarantine was lifted, but before we were married, Katie and I worked it out to go on a road trip by ourselves. We drove from Fort Wayne to Winston-Salem, where my parents lived, and my dad took care of me there while we visited. And then we drove to Nashville, where we met up with some old friends of mine, a married couple who did our engagement photos, and the husband took care of me during that stay. Lastly (or so we thought), we spent a few days with some friends in Chattanooga, and the men there cared for me. Then we hit a snag on the drive back to Fort Wayne and had to make a last-minute stop overnight in Louisville, Kentucky.

One of Katie's best friends from college, Andrea, lived in Louisville with her family. So, Katie called her to have the potentially awkward conversation. Could we stay with them that night? That wasn't the awkward part. They are profoundly kind and generous people, and Katie had stayed with them before. But would her husband, Andy, mind helping Kevan with all of his personal care while we were there?

While they were going to be at our wedding in just a few weeks, and Katie was confident we would get along great because of similar interests, Andy and I had yet to meet. This was quite the introduction to kick off our friendship. But we asked, and Andy said yes. What came out of the next twenty-four hours was something not of this world, a friendship forged in joyful vulnerability and grace.

Looking back on those eight months of engagement, I'm still amazed at how God pulled it off, but Katie and I got to spend almost every day together. Our friendship continued to grow, and we got to enter together into some of my caregiving needs in ways that still honored the Lord and one another. After three wedding plans in two different cities, we ended up getting married at our home church in Fort Wayne exactly one year after our first date and two years after the week we first met.

## Friendship

In his short sermon given during our wedding ceremony, our pastor Ryan quoted C. S. Lewis' book *The Four Loves*: "Friendship . . . is born at that moment when one man says to another: What! You too? I thought that no one but myself . . . "[1] Ryan shared a list of things he and I have in common, including—he pointed out—an affinity for women named Katie (his wife's name as well). He tied it all into the friendship Katie and I have with one another and then the friendships we share with those witnessing our marriage; each has its own "What! You too?" moment, and at the center of them all is Jesus.

But Lewis is clear that these moments are not just the results of similar likes or fun things in common. He says it can be anything "which, till that moment, each believed to be his own unique treasure (or burden)."[2] As we celebrate our shared joys and interests, we can carry one another, too, in our shared burdens and weaknesses. We laugh with one another at birthdays, toast each other upon accomplishments, and weep together in our failures, fears, and frustrations. We walk together across countries, help each other in uncomfortable situations, and invite one another in while the world shuts everyone out in the name of safety. And it is in these experiences that the treasures and burdens we thought were so unique become commonalities because yours become mine, and mine become yours.

## Commonalities

In the account of the early church in Acts, it says that "all who

---

1.    C. S. Lewis, *The Four Loves* (Harper Collins, 1960), 113.
2.    Lewis, *The Four Loves*, 96.

believed were together and had all things in common."[3] And again, "The full number of those who believed were of one heart and soul, and no one said that anything that belonged to him was his own, but they had everything in common."[4]

I have had the joy of witnessing this sense of community firsthand with friends like Luke and Ryan, Andy, Ben, and others. We all want it, don't we? But the answer isn't in a house church, a weekly potluck, a book club, social media, or meeting for coffee. It's a commonality of the heart and soul, which may start with realizing you like the same movies or music but hopefully goes deeper. It's the intentionality of entering one another's needs to such an extent that burdens and treasures become no longer theirs but ours.

When Katie came into my life, my friends stepped up. They had long adopted my needs, but now they went a step further, a step only Lewis' idea of friendship can take. They took on my desires and convictions as well, and by their actions, they said, "What! You too?" They were invested in me being with this girl. Our love story is, in some ways, just as much theirs as it is ours. Katie and I like that.

Our wedding was a beautiful day with my radiant bride. We started the morning in a garden and ended that evening at a feast, reflecting the Wedding Supper of the Lamb, which was our greatest desire for the day. And after months of lockdown, boredom, and anxiety, our friends (including several of my wingmen) danced a conga line with us to a live band playing Bruno Mars' "Uptown Funk," Katie riding on the back of my wheelchair. A year of intentionalities—decisions to share struggles and sacrifices—culminated in commonalities, joy, and freedom. A picture of the Kingdom. Life abundantly.

---

3. Acts 2:44.
4. Acts 4:32.

# CHAPTER NINETEEN

# The Door Needed a Room

*from Tommy*

After Eden but before Easter, there was no hope besides a promise from God that the curse of death was not forever. In that interim, God displayed example after example, glimpse upon glimpse, of how He would ultimately conquer death—by stepping in as our substitute, Himself paying the price to free us from sin.

We see this first in His act of clothing Adam and Eve, who deserved death but were instead covered (literally) by the skins of an animal God killed, the first sacrifice. Next, He made His covenant with Abram. God chose a man, without any merit on Abram's part, to pour out blessing, favor, and purpose.

## Abraham

Now the LORD said to Abram, "Go from your country and your kindred and your father's house to the land that I will show you. And I will make of you a great nation, and I will bless you and make your name great, so that you will be a blessing. I will bless those who bless you, and him who dishonors you I will curse, and in you all the families of the earth shall be blessed."[1]

This was fantastic for Abram; he did nothing to earn and seemingly didn't have to do anything but receive. Not so fast.

And he brought him outside and said, "Look toward heaven, and number the stars, if you are able to number them." Then he said to him, "So shall your offspring be." And he believed the Lord, and he counted it to him as righteousness.[2]

So, faith is a work that credits people with righteousness? I knew there was a catch. Just wait! (But this next part does get weird.) Abram asked God, "How will I *know* that these things will happen?"[3]

He said to him, "Bring me a heifer three years old, a female goat three years old, a ram three years old, a turtledove, and a young pigeon." And he brought him all these, cut them in half, and laid each half over against the other. But he did not cut the birds in half.... As the sun was going down, a deep sleep fell on Abram. And behold, dreadful and great darkness fell upon him.... When the sun had gone down and it was dark, behold, a smoking fire pot and a flaming torch passed between these pieces. On that day the Lord made a covenant with Abram, saying, "To your offspring I give this land."[4]

Abram was not shocked at God's request for rows of animals to

---

1. Gen. 12:1–3.
2. Gen. 15:5–6.
3. Gen. 15:8, paraphrased.
4. Gen. 15:9–10, 12, 17–18.

rend in two. Abram was actually thinking, "Oh, *we* are establishing a covenant! Okay, here we go!" In the time of Abram, when two people made a covenant, they would do this very thing. They cut animals in half, staining the ground red with the blood, then announced the contract and walked between these split animals, a corridor of violence. By doing so, they proclaimed, "To uphold justice, if I fail on my end of our covenant, this is what the other will do to me."

But this was no ordinary covenant, and the ritual would not play out the way it normally did. It says in verse 12 that everything was prepared and Abram was ready to start, but "a deep sleep fell on Abram."[5] It was a covenant-sealing walk with God, and the poor guy fell asleep for it. Abram did not walk through the corridor. He was never supposed to. God put him to sleep and walked through with Himself in the place of Abram. By doing so, He seems to declare that if Abram ever failed to uphold his side of the covenant, God Himself would be torn, and His blood would flow to pay the demand for justice.[6]

From there, He spoke to Abram yet again:

When Abram was ninety-nine years old the LORD appeared to Abram and said to him, "I am God Almighty; walk before me, and be blameless, that I may make my covenant between me and you, and may multiply you greatly." Then Abram fell on his face. And God said to him, "Behold, my covenant is with you, and you shall be the father of a multitude of nations. No longer shall your name be called Abram, but your name shall be Abraham, for I have made you the father of a multitude of nations. I will make you exceedingly fruitful, and I will make you into nations,

---

5. Gen. 15:12.
6. "A Covenant Relationship – Timothy Keller [Sermon]," YouTube, August 10, 2015, https://www.youtube.com/watch?v=xICD5Ycsu04.

and kings shall come from you. And I will establish my covenant between me and you and your offspring after you throughout their generations for an everlasting covenant, to be God to you and to your offspring after you."[7]

Years later in Abraham's life, God came to His friend, and substitutionary blood was spilled again:

God tested Abraham and said to him, "Abraham!" And he said, "Here I am." He said, "Take your son, your only son Isaac, whom you love, and go to the land of Moriah, and offer him there as a burnt offering on one of the mountains of which I shall tell you."[8]

In faith and obedience, Abraham walked his promised one and only son of Sarah to Mount Moriah, where God told him to go. His son, Isaac, asked, "Behold, the fire and the wood, but where is the lamb for a burnt offering?" And Abraham replied, "God will provide for himself the lamb for a burnt offering, my son."[9]

They reached the spot and prepared the altar. I wonder if Abraham had said much, if anything, since that brief comment about God providing. He laid Isaac on the altar and unsheathed his knife, ready to kill if he really had to. But that's when the angel of the Lord showed up! He stayed Abraham's hand and said, "Do not lay your hand on the boy or do anything to him, for now, I know that you fear God, seeing you have not withheld your son, your only son, from me."[10]

---

7. Gen. 17:1–7.
8. Gen. 22:1–2.
9. Gen. 22: 7–8, paraphrased.
10. Gen. 22:12.

The passage goes on to say:

And Abraham lifted up his eyes and looked, and behold, behind him was a ram, caught in a thicket by his horns. And Abraham went and took the ram and offered it up as a burnt offering instead of his son. So, Abraham called the name of that place, "The Lord will provide."[11]

No wonder the Lord guided this father and son to this specific mountain. Our sovereign God had prepared in advance a ram, a grown male lamb, to be caught by thorns crowning his head and offered as a substitutionary sacrifice in the place of Isaac. The ram was ordained; the ram was waiting. This was the mountain of the lamb, and for the lamb to go unseen, the lamb remained silent before his slaughterers until the time came. And when the sacrifice was made, Abraham named the place "The Lord will provide."[12] It has another name, too, but we'll get to that later.

## Passover

Generations passed. Issac, Jacob, Joseph, four hundred years of descendants and slavery later, God again spoke and directed someone to be used for His preordained purpose. He preserved, claimed, and sent Moses to the most powerful nation on earth to be a conduit of God's justice and grace. God Himself would come as an Angel of Death and assault His enemy with the whispering sting of justice. He also covered His people with the grace of a lamb.

---

11. Gen. 22:13–14.
12. Gen. 22:14.

God instructed Moses:

> "Tell all the congregation of Israel that on the tenth day of this month every man shall take a lamb according to their fathers' houses, a lamb for a household. . . . Your lamb shall be without blemish, a male a year old. . . . and you shall keep it until the fourteenth day of this month, when the whole assembly of the congregation of Israel shall kill their lambs at twilight. Then they shall take some of the blood and put it on the two doorposts and the lintel of the houses in which they eat it. They shall eat the flesh that night, roasted on the fire; with unleavened bread and bitter herbs they shall eat it. . . . It is the LORD's Passover. For I will pass through the land of Egypt that night. . . . And when I see the blood, I will pass over you, and no plague will befall you to destroy you, when I strike the land of Egypt. This day shall be for you a memorial day, and you shall keep it as a feast to the LORD; throughout your generations, as a statute forever, you shall keep it as a feast."[13]

The lamb of Passover was the grace of God covering His people with a blood not their own. The body of the lamb was broken, its blood poured out and put on display. The sky darkened. The cries of death shook the homes of those justly punished and passed over the houses of those graciously covered. Liberation followed, and the feast was set as a reminder each year of what God had done and will come to do again.

More time passed, and the feast was lost and found, forgotten and remembered as God's people fell in and out of keeping their covenant with Him. Battles, struggles, kings, kingdoms, rebellions, captivities,

---

13. Ex. 12:3–14.

rescues, more battles, more struggles, the only hope of the world—freedom from death—still lying in a promise. Then an angel showed up and spoke to a virgin. The Baby was born, and the Teacher walked, taught, and healed. Passover came. A room was needed.

As Luke records it, "Then came the day of Unleavened Bread, on which the Passover lamb had to be sacrificed. So, Jesus sent Peter and John, saying, 'Go and prepare the Passover for us, that we may eat it.' They said to him, 'Where will you have us prepare it?'"[14]

And much like His instructions for getting the donkey earlier that week, Jesus said to them:

> "Behold, when you have entered the city, a man carrying a jar of water will meet you. Follow him into the house that he enters and tell the master of the house, 'The Teacher says to you, Where is the guest room, where I may eat the Passover with my disciples?' And he will show you a large upper room furnished; prepare it there." And they went and found it just as he had told them, and they prepared the Passover.[15]

For Jesus to host this feast of remembrance, He needed a room. "Foxes have holes, and the birds of the air have nests,"[16] but the Son of Man had nowhere to set His table. He was about to lay out everything that the previous millennia of covenants and memorial feasts were all pointing to—Himself, paying the price to free us from sin.

This jaunt through the Old Testament we just took together was a path well-worn by Jesus and His twelve disciples. As good Jewish boys, they would have grown up not just observing Passover but knowing the

---

14. Luke 22:7–8.
15. Luke 22:10–13.
16. Matt. 8:20; Luke 9:58.

stories like the backs of their hands and memorizing the Scriptures it all came from. To partake in this feast was profoundly special but not necessarily unique; they did it every year. We can surmise that nothing probably stuck out to them about this particular year's feast, at least not at first, including Jesus' request for them to find a room for it to happen in.

But traditions, like Passover, have two powerful aspects that maybe Jesus leaned into for the sake of His disciples on this special—and hugely unique—occasion. Traditions give us memories as well as a sense of familiarity in their recurrence.

On the night He was betrayed, Jesus gave His disciples a meal to remember Him by. He led them in the tradition, a reminder of God's great faithfulness to Israel, and then washed their feet and spoke truth over them. All of this they could take with them, a comfort upon His death in those dark hours of fear and uncertainty that followed.

But He also used the familiarity of the Passover meal and its understood symbolism to share, in a sense, parables about Himself: "This is my body, broken for you. . . . This is my blood, poured out for you."[17] And although His disciples may not have fully grasped what He was saying until after His resurrection, He had in that room put it all in a context that would set deeply into their hearts when it did click. And these truths, expressed in terms familiar and profound to them, would empower them to live in unparalleled faith and boldness for the gospel for the rest of their lives.

## The Lamb

In the gospel of Mark, Peter recalls that while they were eating the Passover meal, Jesus picked up the bread, broke it, passed it out

---

17. 1 Cor. 11:24–25, paraphrased.

to His disciples, and said, "Take; this is my body."[18] He did the same with the wine, blessing it and passing it around. "This is my blood of the covenant, which is poured out for many. Truly, I say to you, I will not drink again of the fruit of the vine until that day when I drink it new in the kingdom of God."[19]

He proclaimed, if a paraphrase is allowed, "I am the lamb, like the animal that was slaughtered to cover the sin of Adam, like the ram that was slain to graciously spare Isaac, like the spotless lamb whose blood covered your father's grandfather's father's doorpost in Egypt. I am the lamb whose body will be broken and whose blood will be spilled, but I am the Lamb of lambs and the covenant-sealing sacrifice once for all. My time has come, and the place has been picked. See these things and celebrate them by this meal until I come again."

The lamb was caught. The lamb was silent. The lamb was slain. The lamb's blood was smeared on the Roman doorpost of torture. When did it happen? The Gospels tell us it was 3 p.m. Where did it happen? Golgotha, the Place of the Skull, a certain hill outside Jerusalem, a short distance from the temple. Where was the temple built? Tradition tells us it was constructed on Mount Moriah. Where was Abraham led to sacrifice Isaac? Where was the ram found caught in a thicket? A hillside on Mount Moriah. Where was the cross plunged into the ground? Where was the Lamb of God slaughtered? A hillside on Mount Moriah. When? At 3 p.m. The exact time the temple grounds ran red with the blood of Passover lambs. On the very spot where the ram was killed in place of Abraham's son, the Son of God was hung on a tree, the ultimate substitution for all of mankind, to free us from sin and death. What was that other name he gave this hill? In Hebrew, the place Abraham called "The LORD will provide" is also called "On this mountain, He will be seen."

---

18   Mark 14:22.
19   Mark 14:24–25.

Jesus was the Lamb. He was seen. He was slaughtered. We were redeemed.

He needed a room to celebrate Passover, a Rabbi leading His disciples in the beautiful tradition of remembrance. This need Jesus had and expressed was an opportunity to meet the need of a people holding on to an ancient promise. At the Passover dinner in that room, and up a hillside the next day on a cross, Jesus served Himself as the feast of justice and grace. The price of justice paid by His own body for our sake and grace for those covered in His blood.

# CHAPTER TWENTY

# The Man Who Was Wednesday

*from Kevan*

A *Note: One of my favorite authors is G. K. Chesterton. He's famous for a lot of different books, including novels, nonfiction social commentaries, speeches, articles, essays, biographies, and a reluctant memoir. In one of his most well-known novels,* The Man Who Was Thursday, *a set of characters from a secret society are each named after a different day of the week. I would like to employ this tool in the following chapter. The friends I bring up here are not necessarily part of a secret society, but they are part of a community of trust and care, so I would like to protect their privacy by calling them by the days I typically spend with them.*

## The Guys

If you were to drive by our house around 8:30 on a Wednesday morning, you'd see a little red car pull into the driveway. A barefooted man (regardless of the weather) gets out of the car and heads into the house. As the front door shuts, you hear me shout Wednesday's name from down the hall, and he shouts mine right back. Our voices ring out in triumphant joy, like best friends who just found each other on the playground.

Monday mornings are similar, but instead of a red car, it's a black truck at 7:30. This man called Monday has tattoos and intentionally clean sneakers. He and I have a greeting that can be heard across the house, too, as he calls out, "What up?" Half asleep still, I mimic his words and tone but with a shameless yawn in the mix. He comes into the bedroom, and we chat for a bit before he pulls me out of bed and gets me set up on the toilet in the adjoining restroom. Then, he steps back into the bedroom, turns around, and sits on the end of the bed, across from where he has just placed me so that we are face-to-face about five feet apart through a doorway. And so, we continue our conversation.

At the time of writing this, Sunday likes to sit on the end of the bed, like Monday does. Wednesday typically sits in my wheelchair. So does one Friday, while the other Friday (they alternate weeks) does push-ups on the bedroom floor. One Saturday sits on the edge of the tub next to me. The other prefers sitting on the bathroom floor with his back against the wall. Tuesday likes to walk around while we talk. And other guys who fill in (as well as Katie) vary from sitting on the tub to the floor to just walking around the room like Tuesday.

I require a lot of personal care throughout the day: getting ready in the morning, using the toilet, showering, getting dressed, eating, and turning over in bed at night. Most people in my situation hire nurses and aides to help with this sort of stuff. But I've chosen to invite my friends into these needs, and they've stepped up voluntarily to make my life possible. No contracts, no cash, just a handful of guys sharing responsibility, like we're tackling a project together as brothers in Christ.

It isn't always convenient, efficient, or pretty, as my gracious wife can attest. These guys all have jobs, families, and other commitments, so you can imagine the hiccups. Sometimes, they have to swap days, or something comes up at the last minute, and they simply can't make it or have to come at a different time, or our usual amount of time is cut short.

Unfortunately, it sometimes feels like a revolving door too. Guys move, change jobs, or schedules for whatever reason, and they can't make it work anymore. For others, it is simply too much. In a culture of social media, garages, and headphones, the vulnerability of my need can be too much. I can be too much. True or not, those words bounce around in my head: "I'm too much. This won't last. It can't last. I have burned out my friends. I will burn out more of them. They will be emptied, and I will be left all alone."

## A Break

After helping out for just over a year, Wednesday came in one morning, barefoot, of course. I heard the car door shut, then the front door. I called out his name, and he replied with mine, as usual. He brings me a lot of joy and is a good friend to wake up to midweek. He dragged me out of bed and set me on the toilet, then took his place in my wheelchair. Our conversations tend to cover silly stories about his kids, intriguing things we've read in the Bible, entrepreneurial brainstorming, and always ending up on the topic of food. But that day, he looked tired, so I asked him if everything was okay.

The words came tumbling out of him like a landslide, and they were coming from deep inside—concerns for loved ones, time, work, dreams, rest, rhythms. We have grown to be honest with one another, so most of what he said had come up before piece by piece, but to hear it all at once now was overwhelming. Life was heavy on my friend's shoulders, and I could see him breaking under the weight, burning out right in front of me.

When he left that day, Katie and I sat down together to talk through things. We decided that if Wednesday needed a break, we would make sure he got it. Our midweek mornings would be trickier for a bit, but we could figure it out. As long as he was taken care of.

That weekend, I saw him at church.

"Got a minute?" I asked.

Wednesday sat down on the edge of a pew, and I prepared myself for the difficult conversation. That moment when my fears may become realities and the narrative in my head might just prove to be my real-life story. I took in a deep, shaky breath.

"I've been thinking about what you said the other day," I said slowly. "Katie and I talked—and I don't think you were suggesting this or anything—but if you need a break from helping out in the mornings, we want to give that to you."

Wednesday smiled, even laughed.

"Thank you," he said. "That means a lot to me."

It meant a lot to him because he also knew the weight of what it meant for me to offer. My mind went back to our last conversation in these pews a year earlier when I first asked if he would be willing to help out. A mutual friend of ours had stopped helping pretty abruptly, and I had a gaping hole in my schedule—a need—that had to be filled quickly. I had given him a kind of awkward pitch while he sat on the edge of his seat, listening. Before I could finish, he cut in, "Do I get to be part of this?" And now, here we were, a year later, and I was giving him permission to back out.

But he laughed.

"Getting you up on Wednesday mornings is one of the few set rhythms I have in this season of life," he said. "And it's a really life-giving rhythm. So, thank you for the offer—and I will let you know if I ever need it—but that time with you each week is actually really important for me to have right now."

I had a similar conversation with Monday, not long after he started helping. He is a family man, the executive director for a nonprofit, and is invited to speak regularly at enough churches to fill up a year of weekends. He also hosts a house church on Sunday nights, stays active at the YMCA and a local MMA gym, and serves a few dozen widows in his community like they're his own flesh-and-blood mamas. And still, somehow, this guy shows up faithfully every Monday morning to get me out of bed and ready for the day.

Sitting on the end of my bed one morning, he said that his time each week with me was a kind of rest. Because of the nature of my need, my frailty, and lack of balance, he has to be fully present while taking care of me. His usually nonstop world slows down for an hour and a half, and he's forced to slow down with it. At first glance, it may seem like a time full of throwing around a red-headed Muppet from bed to toilet to shower, dry him off, get him dressed, brush his teeth, and so on. But for Monday, it's a time—amidst all that—to breathe and simply be with a friend.

## To Wednesday's Credit

It was Wednesday who first coined the concept of this book. He was praying over me once and thanked God for gifting me with "the hospitality of need." I did a double-take and then let the words sink in. Because I have these weirdly clear needs—to be bathed by others, dressed, and so on—my situation calls for a depth of connection that not many friendships lead to. We all have needs, though, and they beckon us into the same sense of intimacy. The question is whether we will step into those opportunities—that hospitality—so that the needs we have not only *call for* a deeper connection but *foster* it as well.

The guys who say yes—who step into my needs with me—are fed by the experience, time, conversation, a sense of purpose, learning, shaping, laughter, and challenge. I am fed in the same ways and have the same responsibilities as they do as I step into my needs with them. My needs may be what brought us together for the occasion, the door that leads us into the room, but they have needs as well. And just as they are attentive to mine, I must be attentive to theirs. Just as they enter into my needs, I must enter into theirs. For in this case, my needs may be more outward and demanding, but theirs are just as hospitable, and we will find the same depth there together.

I mentioned laughter a moment ago. One of Katie's favorite pastimes is to hear us from the other room in the mornings, goofing off, roughhousing either physically or verbally, and sometimes singing at the top of our lungs. But along with the fun (not aside from it), stepping into one another's needs brings the kind of depth that fulfills something untapped in most of us and grows us up into the men of God we are meant to be. It's the same depth we find as husbands and fathers, but here it is also among friends. It may not be pretty, but it is beautiful. No contracts, no cash, just a handful of guys sharing responsibility, as brothers in Christ.

*Update: The revolving door is very real, but it doesn't have to be necessarily a bad thing. Since writing this chapter, a few guys have come and gone or shifted days. Monday is now on Thursdays, and Tuesday's work schedule has tied up his mornings, but we get together every Tuesday night for Bible study, so we still have quality time . . . even on the same day!*

*A few weeks ago, I was talking with a friend whose son was home from college for the summer. I asked my friend if his son would like to help out in the morning once a week. He asked for more details, so I gave him a rundown of what that usually looks like, and he said he'd talk with his son and let me know. Over the next few weeks, we saw each other at church, a 5K race, and a concert. The conversation never came back up when we saw each other. And then I got a text from my friend one afternoon: "Kevan, do you still need someone on Tuesday mornings? I have been thinking about changing my work schedule." He had decided that, instead of his son, he would accept the invitation for himself!*

*So we have a New Tuesday, if you will. A few weeks after he started, I asked him out of curiosity where that text message came from and why he asked to join the rotation. He shrugged and said, "I didn't really think much about it. I just thought it'd be a great way to spend more time with you." I'm a big fan of that answer.*

# CHAPTER TWENTY-ONE

# Being Present

*from Kevan*

A few years ago, Ben and I were at a conference, and we got to sneak away to visit a local family who had a son in a wheelchair. The dad, a youth pastor with a bright smile, had a tattoo that said "Jesus loves me" in the *Back to the Future* font. You don't get much cooler than that! With two active little boys and a creative daughter, they were a fun, joyful, adventurous family. Mom and Dad were playful, joking with the kids, tossing them around, and Dad was roughhousing with his sons.

There came a point in the evening when it was just the dad and me for a moment, and he asked me a question. "What do you wish someone had told your dad when he was my age?" It was a good question. I had to think about it. Later, when we were leaving their house, I pulled him aside to give an honest answer.

"I wish someone had told my dad that he's my dad for more than just his strength. One day, he'll not be able to take care of me like he used to, but he won't be any less my dad because of it."

I told him I could see how his son looked at him. He loved and respected his dad. He saw him as a superhero and not just because he could throw him around like one. It was because of his character.

His son saw Jesus in him. The boy saw Jesus in his daddy's kindness, faithfulness, and sacrificial love lived out every day. That's what made him a good dad and that doesn't go away with age or strength.

## The Adventures of Kev and Joe

Joe Sutphin introduced himself to me at my first Hutchmoot in 2015, an annual conference put on by the Rabbit Room. Walter Wangerin, Jr. had just finished his keynote speech when a man with a tattered old satchel, spiky hair, and the smirk of a cartoon sat down behind me. He got my attention and said he'd noticed me during the talk. I was hard to miss, sitting on the front row in my wheelchair. Joe had a handful of artwork with him—prints of his illustrations, long before his work on *Little Pilgrim's Progress* and *Watership Down*—and he offered them to me as a gift. My favorite was that of an old, blind rabbit sitting on a log, reading a book of Braille.

We stuck together the rest of the evening and stayed in touch after that. He and his wife, Gina, lived just a few hours from Fort Wayne, so they drove out about a year later for the premier of the *We Carry Kevan* documentary about our Europe trip.

As it turned out, Joe's grandpa was a paraplegic, so Joe grew up around him in a wheelchair, and that familiarity had prompted him to meet me, but our friendship quickly came into its own. The next thing I knew, he was helping with caregiving, and we were traveling buddies! He, Ben, and I were like the Three Musketeers, unstoppable. We drove to Memphis for a film festival, flew to Ft. Lauderdale to attend a charity event, and even spent a week out West once on a speaking tour. It's because of Joe, carrying me in the backpack to a hilltop, that I have experienced the beautiful sight looking down upon the city of Victoria on Vancouver Island.

Once, when he was helping me with the restroom, Joe asked me what my greatest fear was. A much easier question than the one the dad had asked in California. I had my answer ready. My greatest fear was that after all the high-flying fun and adventure, I'd end up alone. As I said it, a sense of relief washed over me. It was the first time I'd said it out loud, and it felt less threatening outside of my head. It was also clear that Joe understood. He had his hand on my shoulder to support me on the toilet, but it became a hand of comfort also as he nodded sadly. What I didn't realize until then was that I had been alone all along in that fear . . . but not anymore.

Joe remembered that conversation, storing it away in his heart, so you can imagine his celebration with me when I met Katie a few years later. How appropriate that it would be Joe and Gina who drove out to Illinois with me to meet Katie's parents for the first time and ask their permission to marry her. And it may come as no surprise, too, that he was one of the groomsmen in our wedding.

But at the time of writing this, due to some recent health issues, Joe has had to forego helping me with caregiving. Lifting me has become a challenge for him, and deadlines with work have made time for him to travel difficult anyway. In some ways, we mourn the loss of our jet-setting days together, but we are finding that the roots of our friendship run deeper than those adventures and physical caregiving. It's a brotherhood of soul care and adventures of the heart, the things that matter most—that matter eternally—and were at the core of our bygone ways all along.

## Personal Presence

In his book *The Tech-Wise Family*, Andy Crouch writes about being with someone on their deathbed when both of you are physically helpless. He says, "When we are at our body's very limits, nothing but personal presence will do."[1] We're not talking in this book, necessarily, about our last breath, but I think the deeper principle applies.

In the case of Joe—and one day, my friend with the *Back to the Future* tattoo—there is only so much we can do for one another physically. But we can still respond to the hospitality of need in each other's lives. We can step into it like a house together and be present. Our world is full of productivity, but what Crouch is getting at is that at the end of the day, it's not the running around or completing projects that will save us; it's the sitting with each other.

I'm forever thankful for friends who carry me on the Great Wall of China (and don't get me wrong, they know me too). But I'm grateful, too, for a friend like Joe, who knows my deepest fears, sorrows, and dreams, and will just sit in them with me. He's not the only one, and each of these friendships is precious to me in its own way.

Responding to the hospitality that can be found in need doesn't have to be some grand expression or movie moment. In fact, more often than not, it will probably be subtle, even missed altogether by the world. Ultimately, it is just saying yes, stepping in, and being present, however that may manifest itself. It sounds easy, and it can be, but I need the reminder of it on a regular basis. Too often, I enjoy these friends' gifts of presence and then wish I could do more physically to bless them in return. But the beauty of a gift of presence like this is that it can be reciprocal in the moment that it's happening. As I heal and grow in my friends' personal presence, they are healing and growing in mine as well. And nothing else will do.

## Time Together

One of my favorite memories is of spending a summer afternoon

---

1. Andy Crouch, *The Tech-Wise Family: Everyday Steps for Putting Technology in Its Proper Place* (Baker Books, 2017), 203.

exploring with Joe in the field behind his house. It came at a heavy time in my life when it felt like a lot of dreams I had were coming apart at the seams, and I was consumed with frustration. Joe was going through a hard season as well, and our wives decided we needed a day together to heal in each other's presence.

We talked a little bit about the things on our minds, but mostly, we just meandered in nature. He walked patiently beside my bumbling wheelchair. A thick staff hung loose in his hand, and he used it to point out plants and critters along the path he had mowed just the day before. I got to witness firsthand the miracles that give life to his imagination and inspire the artwork so many of us have come to know and love from him. And together, we healed.

A few months later, we found out we would both be in Nashville at the same time. He was there for a conference, while Katie and I were there for some meetings. There were a few other mutual friends in town for the conference, too, so we made plans to all gather where Katie and I were staying.

There was just one catch. As Katie and I wrapped up our meetings and the guys finished at the conference, we started texting back and forth to work out the details. What was the address? Who all was coming? Did we want to get pizza, or just snacks? Amid the planning, Joe let us know he wouldn't be able to make it. He was down to the wire on a big project; he had to work on it every free second and just couldn't get away.

I called him as soon as the text came in. The call was short. He sounded miserable, like a kid who'd been grounded from going to his friend's birthday party. I prayed with him, assured him we understood, and said we'd miss him.

The other guys arrived, with Oreos and chips in hand. Conversations kicked off and went in a hundred different amazing directions within the first five minutes. Between stories, our friend Sam checked his phone and said, "Oh cool, Joe will be here in a bit!" Later, we found out Joe had called Gina back home and she'd encouraged him to come hang out. He needed time with his friends. Meeting a deadline was one thing, but meeting it with his sanity still intact was another. He flew into the room that night like that grounded kid was set free. And while most of the night, he just sat quietly and listened, the tired smile on his face told me he was right where he needed to be.

# CHAPTER TWENTY-TWO

# The Beginning Needed a Tomb

*from Tommy*

J esus borrowed a tomb to be buried, and its owner, Joseph of Arimathea, was greatly blessed. As we have seen, Jesus always used His needs as invitations. For Joseph then and us now, the blessing Jesus shares in His burial is the invitation to be buried in Him. And those buried in Jesus will share in the blessing of rising with Him to life, never needing a tomb in death. What a sweet truth we have to proclaim!

A frequent refrain of prayer from the pulpit of my congregation is, "God, preach through me if you would, around me if you must, but please preach, and give us ears to hear." God certainly doesn't *need* a preacher through whom to preach. God has quite a set of pipes Himself, and Scripture even points out that all of creation declares His glory just fine too. No, God doesn't *need* a preacher, but He often borrows one to sow the seeds of truth.[1] It's an odd thought, God borrowing. But the mouth of the preacher through whom to speak, a womb in which to be woven, a well from which to drink, penitent tears by which to

---

1. Rom. 10.

wash, a donkey for triumphant entry, a spare room to share the Passover, and a tomb in which to be buried, all borrowed, all a need met and a blessing shared.

In the realm of needs had and needs satisfied, the need of Jesus for a tomb wasn't met by Jesus asking. In the Gospels we never see Jesus inviting a disciple close to whisper, "I have one last favor to ask." Jesus only alluded to His burial in two unlikely ways. One odd reference was to a seed falling to the ground and dying. And the other was when having just had His feet washed in tears and anointed with perfume, Jesus said the woman's service had prepared Him for it.

Jesus knew He needed to be buried. He knew all the details of *how* He needed it to happen but never expressed those needs or asked anyone to meet them. So, there is something uniquely powerful in the way Jesus, in His divine sovereignty, must have planted this need in the heart of Joseph and simply knew he would meet it. We are always grateful when someone joyfully answers the call to meet a need. But how humbling and uplifting it can be when someone loves us enough to anticipate a need and meet it.

The weight of Jesus' need for burial went far beyond anything logistical and material. There was a beautiful depth of need etched in stone long before His tomb was even cleft. Much like the need of Jesus to ride into Jerusalem on a borrowed burro to fulfill prophecy, the need for a borrowed tomb was also penned by a prophet. And prophecy must be fulfilled because if it isn't, it wasn't a prophecy.

> And they made his grave with the wicked
> and with a rich man in his death.[2]

---

2. Isa. 53:9.

Six hundred years later:

When it was evening, there came a rich man from Arimathea,
named Joseph, who also was a disciple of Jesus. He went to Pilate
and asked for the body of Jesus. Then Pilate ordered it to be given
to him. And Joseph took the body and wrapped it in a clean linen
shroud and laid it in his own new tomb, which he had cut in the
rock. And he rolled a great stone to the entrance of the tomb and
went away.[3]

## Generosity of a Man

Joseph of Arimathea was a wealthy man, a man of the Sanhedrin,
but also an unlikely and secret follower of Jesus. This man had more to
risk than the known disciples who hid or Peter who lied about knowing
Jesus. It was not open knowledge that Joseph sympathized with Jesus'
teachings, or perhaps even believed the Pilate-ordered inscription
above Jesus' head: "This is the King of the Jews."[4] Joseph didn't stand
to gain any profit from meeting this need that Jesus had. Quite to the
contrary, he spent and put on the line a profound amount of his own
treasures, position, legacy, and a measure of eternity to provide for Jesus'
burial. Above and beyond that, Joseph had no inkling of consideration
in his actions that the offering up of his own burial tomb was merely
a loan to Jesus, not a gift.

Joesph of Arimathea, in giving away the place for his bones or
even sharing the place with an accused heretic, hazarded the value of
his name and risked his own eternity. This was not just doing someone
a favor; it was sacrificing everything he is in order to bestow honor
upon another. Without being asked (as far as we know), and costing

---

3. Matt. 27:57–60.
4. Luke 23:38.

the security of his place in the life to come, he stood from his seat and offered it to the bones of Jesus. If his motivation was genuine love and saving faith, I take great joy in imagining what was in store for Joseph. Picture Joseph's eternal delight when he discovered his gift was only briefly borrowed and that his own bones would be next to borrow the tomb on the great day to come when he joined the thief with Jesus in paradise. There is measureless life to be found in giving it away.

Jesus was crucified with the wicked and then buried in the place of the wealthy. He had no wickedness to deserve death or wealth to purchase a tomb, so He needed a loan of both. "For our sake he made him to be sin who knew no sin, so that in him we might become the righteousness of God."[5] And even if Jesus had the money, tombs aren't refundable or rented by the day. Jesus would never be the permanent resident of a grave, so He had no need for one of His own. He didn't owe a debt of death like the rest of sinful man, so He embraced death on loan as well. He was wrapped in burial garments, but the burial clothes were not His to keep either, and He left them behind, folded up on the bed like a polite guest might leave a borrowed bathrobe.

## Burial of a King

Before sending Jesus to the cross, Pilate asked Him if He was the King of the Jews, and Jesus didn't argue with him. King Jesus was crucified on the cross and needed to be buried. The prophet Isaiah had something to say about the burial of kings. They were laid in their own tombs, made just for them, and there they remain still. "All the kings of the nations lie in glory, each in his own tomb."[6]

Isaiah said the Messiah would be laid in a borrowed tomb—on loan, not kept. Jesus is the only person who borrows a tomb and returns

---

5. 2 Cor. 5:21.
6. Isa. 14:18.

it, and even tidies up the place before He leaves. But it is not as though His death was less than full or His burial was less than complete. He didn't just pass out or swoon; He died a gruesome, public, and horrible death. And contrary to the protests of those who doubt His resurrection, His body was not buried in a shallow grave to be easily stolen or hidden. He was buried deeply and completely in the maw of death, sealed with the weight of a stone, and guarded by the might of Rome.

The substance and manner of His burial left no doubt in the minds of His enemies and in the hearts of His friends. Jesus was all (not just mostly) dead. People either rejoiced or despaired, but no one was unsure. Perhaps the earthquake at that hour shook Jesus' words from the memory of those who mourned Him and were thus no comfort to them. He had said, "Truly, truly, I say to you, unless a grain of wheat falls into the earth and dies, it remains alone; but if it dies, it bears much fruit."[7]

## Planting of a Seed

The truth that Jesus declared of the fruit blooming from the buried seed does not exist only to comfort those in the wake of death but to raise up those who are in Christ. Even higher still, the resurrection of those found in the Lamb, buried and raised, has been the plan from the beginning:

> The earth brought forth vegetation, plants yielding seed according to their own kinds, and trees bearing fruit in which is their seed, each according to its kind. And God saw that it was good. And there was evening and there was morning, the third day.[8]

---

7. John 12:24.
8. Gen. 1:12–13.

Throughout Scripture, we see that God purposed the first creation from the beginning to be a revelation of the coming glory of the resurrection and re-creation. Jesus said that the seed must be buried and die to bear fruit. In His resurrection, Jesus Himself was raised from the ground as fruit from a seed, which was the design planted in creation on the third day of it.

And what sprang forth from the seed that was planted? Not just one fruit from one seed but an exponential harvest from one borrowed tomb. In trying to appreciate the truth that both the served and the one serving share in blessing, it is not hard to understand this example, but it may be hard to grasp its magnitude. It is clearly not *only* Joseph of Arimathea who was blessed by his gift. We who rejoice in the risen Lord all share in the blessing of Joseph's hospitality to the bones of Jesus as we are welcomed into the body of Christ.

# CHAPTER TWENTY-THREE

# The Bread of Life Needed a Snack

*from Tommy*

n His first resurrected encounter with the disciples, the formerly dead
Jesus walked through the wall of their hiding place and asked them
for a snack. "Have you anything here to eat?"[1] And sure enough,
they did! Luke goes on to say they gave Him a piece of broiled fish
and some honeycomb.

I love that Jesus decided to ask for food. Imagine you're one of
the disciples. Consider the rugby scrum of emotions you would have
been thrown into at that moment. Shock, disbelief, belief, relief, and
many questions, but you also want to leap to your feet and make the
man a sandwich.

No. Something fancier.

A deconstructed open-face broiled fish sandwich (hold the bun)
with locally sourced artisanal honey on the side as a palette cleanser.
You want it to be nice, but you also want it to be quick because you
don't want to pull a Martha and be stuck in the kitchen for too long.

---

1. Luke 24:41.

You want to be in the presence of your friend and teacher who has now proven also to be your Lord.

But wait, as you're plating the fish and breaking the comb, the thought occurs to you again: Why does a man, who is God, who died and is now alive, need a snack? If His body conquered the grave, does His body still succumb to the nibbles? You even recall when you encouraged Jesus to eat, and He replied that His food was to do His Father's will, which He came to complete.

Pause. Eyes widen.

He did complete it!

## Resurrection

In Jesus' asking for food, the disciples were given a gift they thought had been lost. Serving Jesus was what they thought they were born to do. A purpose and identity they thought had died with Him. This was the first taste of a new reality. It is not only Jesus who is resurrected; it is Jesus who is the resurrection itself.[2] Disciples are buried with Christ so that "just as Christ was raised from the dead by the glory of the Father, we too might walk in newness of life."[3] It is the old self that dies, not the whole self. Like iron melted and refined in the crucible and then cast into a new form, only the dross is cast aside; nothing of value is lost, just reshaped, reforged, and repurposed. Christians are redeemed and reformed in the death and resurrection of Jesus, not wiped out and replaced. Jesus told John the Revelator, "Behold, I am making *all* things new."[4] What if need itself is part of all those things that are made new?

Is it possible that, when we look ahead to "shuffling off this mortal

---

2.   John 11:25.
3.   Rom. 6:4.
4.   Rev. 21:5.

coil,"[5] some of the heavenly glory we imagine and hope for is tied to a fantasy of not needing anything and no one needing anything from us? I wonder if, in eternity, we who are in His glorious resurrection will experience a transformation of our relationship with need. In this life, we have needs. In the life to come, we may still have needs. But those needs won't be manifested nor fulfilled out of any sort of broken necessity. No, they will be derived from and met by the Christ-centered, Christ-afforded, Christ-provided, Christ-glorifying opportunity to worship Him in fellowship: what we were created for in the first place.

John is shown the consummation of something gloriously long-promised. A wedding feast. The Lamb is the groom; His church is the bride. We are the bride. And we will feast for the joy set before us. In the sweetness of His fellowship, set to the harmony of every tongue singing His praise, we will swap stories of how He filled us and exalt Him because He fills us still. Our first glimpse of this future reality is not in the Revelation written by John, but in a piece of broiled fish perhaps served by that beloved disciple himself.

## Fellowship

Hiding away in that room, the disciples were gathered together, pressed down in the aftermath of their Rabbi's very public death. They were probably sitting in the ashes of grief, silence, confusion, regret, and fear. And then, Jesus, having completed the work His Father sent Him to do, stepped in, sat down, and asked for a plate. His request had to be such a beautiful assurance to them that they weren't seeing things. This wasn't a ghost. This was Jesus, back from the dead, alive and well, in the flesh.

Think about it: The resurrected Christ could do anything with

---

5. *Hamlet*, William Shakespeare, paraphrased.

His time and presence. If He could appear in upper rooms, He could surely have appeared in Pilate's chambers, the council of Pharisees, or before astonished crowds and demanded to be lifted high. Instead, He went to His friends and lifted them. Can we hazard to wonder about the stirrings of Jesus' heart as He saw the fulfillment His disciples experienced in meeting the needs of their Rabboni, who was dead but now alive? I wish I could have seen the perfect smile on His face as He looked ahead further to the resurrection still in store for these blessed friends whom the Father had given Him.[6] But at this moment, to soothe their aching need for hope and the assurance of resurrection, He asked for them to feed Him. He gifted them an opportunity to offer the hospitable gesture of refreshment for a guest who just dropped by.

---

6. John 17:6–12.

# CHAPTER TWENTY-FOUR

# True Communion

## *from Kevan*

I love taking Communion. Whether it's in a church, living room, or BBQ restaurant, one of my favorite things in the world to do is practice the Lord's Supper with fellow believers. It's not just something Jesus commanded us to do. It's something we know for a fact His disciples did, too, just like us. He introduced them to it in the upper room, just before His death and resurrection. We have it recorded in the Gospels that Jesus Himself passed out the bread, saying, "This is my body, broken for you," and then the cup, saying, "This is my blood, poured out for you." The disciples heard this, and then ate and drank.[1]

Paul brings it up, too, in one of his letters to the Corinthians.[2] Years, maybe a couple decades, after the disciples first did it, the church was doing it too. So, when we take Communion together today, we are doing what they did and for the same reasons—to proclaim the Lord's death until He returns, and by so doing, growing closer to Him and to one another.

In early-1800s Ireland, there was a group of men who were unhappy with the mainstream church and it's growing obsession with

---

1. Matt. 26:26–29; Mark 14:22–25; Luke 22:14–23.
2. 1 Cor. 11:23–26.

program, pomp, and circumstance. These men began meeting in each other's homes, to share what they were learning in their personal Bible reading and to take Communion together. Simple. Focused. They became known as the Plymouth Brethren. Just a few years later, my great-great-grandfather, William Payne, was introduced to Jesus in one of these meetings, and so I guess you could say I come by this affection honestly.

## Getting Close

I love taking Communion, and the peace that washes over me in the process—a cleansing flood like I can't seem to find anywhere else. As I eat the bread and drink the cup, I know the presence of Christ. I sense His nearness, feel His touch. He comes down my way and pulls me up toward Him, the chasm between us shrinking to a sliver under His mighty footstep.

Heaven comes close, if only for a second, and in that second if we are doing Communion right—repentant and with others—we find we are not alone in the sweet revelation. Using Jewish bridegroom language, Jesus instructed us with Communion to await His return. So, we wait as one and, in our waiting, experience together a glimpse of the Kingdom. It is, among other things, a foretaste of the cleverness of God that we will get to delight in for eternity.

My dad's Bible was large, war-torn, and lay open like a map in his broad hands. I sat next to him, soaking in the quiet at six years old, at fifteen, at thirty. You could feel it every Sunday morning. Pages turning of Scripture and hymn books all around me sounded like ocean waves in the holy stillness. This room was different from the rest of the world, and it had something to do with that bread and cup on a table in the middle.

Someone shared a Bible verse, and another prayed. With a muffled cough, someone shifted in their seat. "Hymn number . . ." was called out for us all to sing, then quiet again before the bread was passed out and eaten. *This is my body, broken for you.* More quiet. Peace, the kind that passes understanding. Another hymn or two, a prayer. Sometimes, my dad would stand and read aloud a passage from that old, war-torn Bible. Then, the cup. *This is my blood, poured out for you.* I found rest in that quiet, surrounded by a fortress of truth spoken and sung by the giants of faith around me. And then, I got to share in Communion with them, like Mephibosheth at David's table, feasting alongside the mighty men.[3]

## My Weakness

I love taking Communion because of all it means to the past, future, and right now, internally between me and God and socially with my brothers and sisters in Him. It can be wine or juice, yeast rolls or gluten-free crackers. Whatever the menu, with the right hearts, we get to participate in praise and adoration, reflection, repentance, celebration, and hope, all in one simple, sacred action. The full encapsulation of worship and a glimpse of the Kingdom happen in this brief moment as we eat and drink together.

So, you can imagine how my heart was broken when I could no longer take Communion. Rather, I couldn't serve myself Communion. My disease is progressive, and in my mid-thirties, not long before meeting Katie, the muscles in my good arm (my left one) decided the distance to my mouth was too far to go anymore, and my wrist decided the same. I could still use a fork for some meals, but to hold a small piece of bread between my fingers and deliver it to my lips was definitively out of the question. If my arm managed to bend that far upward, my wrist gave out and went down, much like an excavator.

I didn't mind asking for help. Deacons, pastors, and friends were

---

3. 2 Sam. 9:11b.

all willing. But it wasn't the same. This was a precious act to me, the most precious and personal. And now I felt that I had to sacrifice its importance to me. If no one was there to help, I had to kindly decline the elements offered to me, though it destroyed me inside. If someone could help, that sweet time of reflection had to be spent on those wallet-dropping questions I wrestled with on the sidewalk outside. What had been my favorite pastime of worship for thirty years suddenly became the thing I most feared and missed all at once. And then Katie came along.

## Katie

As I write this, my precious wife is working in the front garden. She is planting lavender and training our clematis to grow on the trellis. Their green leaves brighten at her touch, and every neighbor who passes by stops to chat. It is a chance to be seen by Katie today and loved by her. They walk away refreshed, full of hope and sunshine. I know the feeling well. Her delight in me every day brings me to life.

Every winter, my muscles get heavy with the cold. Last winter, I had an especially hard night when my arms felt like they were full of lead and just wouldn't move. To try to warm me up, Katie and I made soup for dinner. When we make soup, my job is to stir and give instructions on what spices to put in. But tonight, I couldn't. My good arm was just too heavy—useless. I gave up and sat at the stove with my arms in my lap while Katie leaned against me and took over stirring.

We were listening to the gospel song "There's a Leak in This Old Building." It was the tipping point for me, hearing the words that fit exactly what I felt. I broke down in tears, burying my face in Katie's shoulder.

"My building's leaky, Katie," I sobbed.

She held me and cried, too, feeling my pain to her core. The soup could wait. She squeezed me tight, wrapping me in both arms, as I shook uncontrollably. Then she spoke. And while I heard my wife's sweet voice, I heard the voice of Jesus too.

"I love your old building, Kevan. I love it, leaks and all."

## My Gift

So, back to my struggle with taking Communion. My muscles wouldn't let me lift the bread to my mouth, let alone the cup. It's called Communion because we all take it together, but I felt a disconnect by my limitations. When we started going to church together, Katie helped me take it, and I was grateful for the consistency again and to be taking it with her. This was healing enough for me. But our Father in Heaven has a way of giving good gifts to His kids, gifts we never saw coming and never knew could be so good.

One morning, maybe a year into our marriage, Katie and I were sitting in church. The congregation was invited to come down, get the bread and cup, and take it back to their seats for us all to take together. The ushers offered to bring the elements to Katie and me. So, we sat quietly, waiting as our friends went down front and then returned to their seats, some passing our way to say hi. Katie patiently held our wafers and juice. I eyed them in her hands.

"Hey," I whispered. "Can I hold that?"

I pointed to one of the wafers. She nodded and held it up for me to pinch between my thumb and forefinger (my two strongest fingers). She gave me a curious look, but I just grinned and settled back into waiting. Holding the juice would be a bad idea all around, so I'd leave that to her, but I had an idea about the bread. I just wondered if it could work.

Everyone was seated at last.

"On the night He was betrayed," the elder said from the pulpit. "Jesus took the bread."

I just wondered.

"And giving thanks, He broke it, saying, 'This is my body broken for you.'"

Katie lifted the wafer in her hand to her own mouth but looked to see how I was doing. Would I get mine up to my mouth? But that wasn't my aim. I couldn't feed myself, but I wondered. As she looked over, she saw I was holding the wafer out to her, albeit a little low. My wife smiled softly, leaned down, and accepted it, letting me feed her the body broken for her. And she, in turn, fed me the wafer in her hand.

And this act of worship, done together, redeems our frailties and shortcomings, just as His adoption of us has "redeemed our bodies," as Paul puts it to the Romans.[4] As I serve the bread to Katie each Sunday now, and she serves me, I feel that redemption in my bones and my soul. I feel a mysterious wholeness. What the world sees—what I have seen—as my weakness has ushered me into and outfitted me for this priesthood, to love my bride as Christ loved the church and to serve her as He served His disciples in that upper room. So, we commune in holy matrimony, carrying one another to the feet of Jesus by this act of taking the bread and cup together *in remembrance*.

## Together

I love taking Communion for the gathering we are called into around it. Brennan Manning once wrote, "The Good News of the gospel of grace cries out: we are all, equally, privileged but unentitled beggars at the door of God's mercy!"[5] And as I approach Communion with my brothers and sisters, as we step toward the elements or they are brought to us, I see us standing together at that door. It's precisely because we are beggars that we get to stand at that door. Our need for

---

4. Rom. 8:23, paraphrased.
5. Brennan Manning, *The Ragamuffin Gospel* (Multnomah, 2000), 27.

God *is* the door to His mercy, isn't it? Every day, I am more and more convinced of this as I realize just how beggarly I am and how truly desperate we all are for Him. I realize it, in one sense, by my lack, by the ache that I feel deep inside, and in another much greater sense, I realize it by that very lack being filled to brimming with the love of Jesus as He opens the door and welcomes us in.

By the grace of God, I have witnessed broken people joining in the act of Communion, carrying one another to the table, myself counted among them. Homeless people stagger forward for a taste, a dad who recently lost his child weeps as he walks, recovering addicts celebrate a year of sobriety as they reach for a little cup of juice, deaf people, blind people, the elderly, the orphaned, the weary and heavy-laden, and the cripple. Our needs lead us through the open door of God's mercy into the Kingdom of Heaven. We get to see glimpses of this Kingdom every day through our care for one another and our bearing up one another as we move toward it, carried by His cords of kindness.

One day, we will all enjoy it together, children of God from every tribe, tongue, nation, and maybe even need. We will celebrate the Wedding Feast at a big table with the Samaritan woman, the disciples, Joesph of Arimathea, Chesterton, Lewis, Nouwen, Rich Mullins, a couple of my homeless friends, and maybe even the boatman who waited for us on Skellig Michael. And as we take that bread and cup, Jesus, for the first time since the upper room, will take it with us.

Until that day, let us share in our needs together, much like we share in Communion. They are, after all, foretastes of the age to come, when we gather at last to rest and feast in the full presence of our Lord. Hungry, we will be filled by His body broken; thirsty, we will be slaked by His blood poured out. Even now, He is preparing us for that sweet reality as we heal and grow together in the gift He's given us: the hospitality of need.

# From the Rooftop

*from Tommy*

My father is a pastor, and I grew up as a very proud pastor's son. Week after week, he preached the truth that he lived out at home. My father is a tender and faithful under-shepherd of Jesus' flock. He visited the shut-ins, bringing them the sacraments of Communion and the fellowship of the body of Christ. I kind of thought he slept with his shirt and tie on because how else would he have made it on time to hold Miss Channing's hand as she passed at 3:26 in the morning?

When I was twelve, I watched my grandfather (on my dad's side) walk down the tiny hallway of their little home on Spinway Place the day my grandmother passed away. He had taken care of her for decades in her crippling diabetic infirmity. His once striking figure was slumped and pale in his grief. As sad as it was, I knew my nanny was with Jesus, and after such an exhausting marathon of caregiving, I assumed that he would actually have a sense of relief. My pop-pop's words in that hallway were, "It wasn't enough time." It seems his decades of labor were decades of joy; and to him, they were too short.

When Pop-Pop had a stroke and couldn't take care of his own needs anymore, my father brought him into our home. I was as selfless and wise as any seventeen-year-old is and only tangentially connected to caring for the man. I was busy. It was messy. But I was there to watch, as a son, my father cared for his father without fault. My father disagrees, but he's wrong. I was home alone with my grandfather one day, and he had a very embarrassing accident in the bathroom. I tried to clean it up but got overwhelmed. I called my father, and he raced home. I apologized for not being able (willing) to put my grandfather and our bathroom back together. My dad responded, "He's my father. It's my job." I now know what he meant was, "He's my daddy. It's my honor." When Pop-Pop passed, what were the words that overflowed from my father's heart? "It wasn't enough time."

Years later, when the health and vitality of my mother's parents began to fade, I was again stirred by watching my mom and dad take their turns to faithfully "honor father and mother," which, in the Bible hidden in my dad's heart, very much includes mother and father-in-law.[1] As my grandparents stepped closer to their time written in the Book, my parents, for months and months, took turns on leaves of absence from their professional lives to abide with my grandparents, taking care of their every need. But more needs were met than bathing, housekeeping, and feeding. Whenever I heard my mother say, "Yes, Daddy, what do you need?" I could just sense the decades of their complicated relationship molt off like scales and be replaced with mending joy.

When my "Lady" and "Grandfather" passed away, four months apart from each other, after sixty-five years of marriage and seventy-seven years of best-friendship, my dad called down the steps. "Tommy, your mother needs you." I knew what had happened in the early hours of that morning, the day before Thanksgiving. I had sat on

---

1. Ex. 20:12, paraphrased.

the corner of her bed the night before and watched joy beam through her tired face as I introduced her to our baby Nora. After the longest climb of those familiar basement steps, I watched my father carry my grandmother's body with gentle honor through the doorways and outside to the attendants from the funeral home. As my sister and I held our mother, what do you suppose reverberated through her heart? "It wasn't enough time."

All of these are picture windows into moments of my past as a spectator of need, but also a portal into the future, when it will be my turn to step into it for my parents and those of my wife. I have inherited a legacy of faithfully and joyfully meeting need. Their examples have given me no choice but to follow. Jesus has shown me, by heart and sight, no other way. I have no choice, but not because I fear breaking a rule or falling short of a standard. I just have no other choice, and I don't want one. What I cannot "un-know" is that choosing to pass on need is passing on joy. I can see the moment approaching when it will be my turn to say, "Yes, Daddy, what do you need?" and "There wasn't enough time."

How could anyone want more time to change their parent's diapers, more time to feed them, more time to witness them change day after day, more time to be and feel powerless to stop an abiding relationship from slipping into something different and unknown? Why would someone want more time for that? Well, doesn't every parent say about their children, with joy and sorrow: "They grow up too fast." We always want more time for joy. Perhaps a parent inviting a child to care for them as they die is a gracious invitation to pay back the joy of caring for them when they were born.

Five and a half years ago, I stepped into shepherding ministry like my dad did forty years prior, and with his towering example before me, I started praying, "Lord, I know that I will do the right thing. I know when the phone rings, I'll do it. I'll follow my dad's example as he has followed Yours. Jesus, I know I'll do it. But I don't want to do it just because it's the right thing to do. I want to do it because I desire to do it. I want to have joy, real joy, in serving. I want to respond to the joy of obedience and humility, not obligation."

And then Kevan Chandler invited me into this crazy thing. I gladly stepped in with my proprietary blend of overconfidence and looming failure, and throughout the first months, I tried to give Kevan endless "outs." And all Kevan would say is, "Just keep writing." And so several billion rambling words later, a new chapter of the story began. I was invited to enter into Kevan and Katie's need, and they were hospitable. They were traveling between a few events, and I was able to step into all of Kevan's needs. All of them. And I was right, when he asked me on the phone if I would be willing, I was, absolutely. I knew what he was asking of me, and I faithfully agreed. But was it joy? Did I greet the opportunity with thanksgiving? My words and my heart danced, but maybe not to the same music.

Then something happened, though I didn't notice when. Jesus had apparently planted some seeds of joy that sprouted somewhere between the carrying and the toilet. And it struck me that Jesus was answering my prayer. I had begun to find great joy in meeting my brother's needs, and it wasn't by white knuckles; it was a joyful, blessed desire. Sometimes, writing a book results in more than a book.

Kevan invited me to lower him through a "roof," as it were. And I don't know about the paralytic's friends in the gospel accounts, but I know myself and what I've seen through the hole in this particular roof, and it has changed me forever. I didn't know what the seeds were when God's sovereign hand planted them throughout my short forty-five, but I know what He has done in the last couple of years coauthoring this book. He has shown me that those seeds and this book were ordained to answer a prayer I hadn't even prayed yet. How? Well, I pray that this book perhaps answers that question. Or maybe we could just ask Kevan; it was the hospitality of his need that invited me into this anyway. All I did was say yes. Jesus is sneaky like that.

# Where We Go from Here

As Kevan and Tommy have helped us to see so vividly, need is not merely a lack, an emptiness. It is also a *place*. It is *the* place, like a dance floor, where receiving and giving can join, awkwardly at first but steadily learning to move together in shared rhythms, intimate and bound to one another.

We often fear these places, where the smell of others' need is pungent, perhaps literally so. We may fear even more to tread where our own need may be nakedly exposed. Such spaces are not fit for polite company.

And yet, so much of what we most long for can be found nowhere else.

I see this reality again and again in my daily work in the Christian Alliance for Orphans. Whether through foster care or adoption or other expressions of love, courageous families welcome children who've lacked protection and care. This welcoming-of-need begets other need. When a family receives a child who has known great hurt, they most always share in that hurt too. Meanwhile, they're also dealing with broken government systems and often do their best to help a child's biological parents as well. It's more than one family can sustain on its own.

This overwhelming need, however, becomes an invitation. It beckons others in their church to press beyond polite coffee-and-donuts fellowship and into true Christian fellowship, what the Bible calls *koinonia*. When that invitation is answered, it begins a cascade of life together that many believers had never experienced before.

I can still see the day a baby appeared suddenly in my family through foster care. He'd arrived much sooner than expected, born eight weeks early due to drug exposure. There we were, wide-eyed, an unanticipated newborn in my wife's arms, wondering how we'd do it, already raising our five children and a full life besides. Our youngest daughter was three, so we no longer possessed any of the equipment thought to be so essential to babyhood these days.

But word spread quickly among friends from church. First one, then another, showed up at our house—with diapers and rash cream, a car seat, teensy-tiny onesies, and a marvelous diaper genie. Others brought meals. We received two full dinners that first evening. Over the months ahead, those gifts kept coming, along with help running errands, babysitting, and more. Each gift met a practical need. Even more, they told us we weren't in it alone. Thread by thread, small acts of care wove a deep sense of connectedness and mutual affection, true *koinonia*.

That word is a beautiful one. It's often translated as *fellowship*, and rightly so. But we over-busy, self-sufficient moderns tend to water down its biblical strength. We imagine pleasant people milling about in a church foyer, sipping coffee and trading words.

That's not a terrible place to start. But the vision Scripture casts includes much more. Horizontally, *koinonia* spans from shared meals and simple hospitality to active partnership in sharing the gospel to sacrificial financial gifts to meet others' needs.[1] Vertically, it encompasses

---

1. Acts 2:42; Phil. 1:6; Rom. 15:26; 2 Cor. 8:4; Heb. 13:16.

the marvel and mystery of our union with God in Christ.[2] Paul even describes a *koinonia* "of sharing in [Christ's] sufferings."[3]

This marvelous and many-threaded weaving of lives is among the most precious things humans can experience. Anyone who's felt it— even in the imperfect forms we tend to find on earth—knows that Kevan and Tommy were speaking truth in describing its sweetness. As they expressed, it overflows with healing, comfort, rest, adventure, and joy. That's not wishful thinking or salesmanship, my friends. It comes from a man in a wheelchair and a pastor who have tasted the things of which they speak.

God does not invite us into all this merely as a problem-solving strategy. To live immersed in *koinonia* is—like all of God's ways—pro-foundly *good for us*. Indeed, this hospitality of need presents an antidote to much of what most ails modernity. It is strong medicine, matched perfectly for the great lacks and longings of our present moment.

*The hospitality of need is an antidote for isolation.* We ache to be-long but do not understand that belonging is woven, especially with countless threads of mutual responsibility and sacrifice. Caring for others' needs and sharing our own knits us together as nothing else can. It draws us out from the lonely dens where we peer at the world and others through screens. Caregiving demands face-to-face, hand-to-hand, touch and sweat, and sometimes blood. It wakes us from our device-fed stupor and puts an end to our tragic seclusion.

*The hospitality of need is an antidote for self-centeredness.* The dance of giving and receiving takes us in precisely the opposite direction of selfishness and its pitfalls. It reorients not only our outward actions but also, critically, our thought life too. Any mindset, counselor, or therapy that turns our attention mainly to ourselves will yield only anxiety and

---

2.   1 Cor. 1:9; 10:16; 2 Peter 2:4.

3.   Phil. 3:10 NIV.

unhappiness in the long run. Solely in lifting our eyes beyond ourselves, to God and to others, are we freed from the terrible burden of self-focus. In Christ, we trade it for the light yoke of self-forgetfulness.

*The hospitality of need is an antidote for shallow, impotent Christianity.* Whenever we follow Jesus into one another's need, joining Him there in the dance of mutual care, we never emerge the same. We are formed anew, especially by small choices frequently repeated, steadily growing more like Jesus.

No, this is not the good life, nor an easy one. *But it is the best life.* If that's what we desire, where do we begin?

As Kevan and Tommy express plainly, nothing in all they shared started with them. It flowed from the heart of God Himself. We love, ever and always, because He first loved us.[4] God's hospitality is the wellspring of ours.

So, it makes all the sense in the world to go first to the source—looking to Him, soaking in His life, asking for clarity as to the particulars of what and how, and for the strength to do it well. All of that can be summed up in a word: prayer.

Making that more personal, after reading this book, I've sensed God leading me toward two requests in particular. First, that God would help me to see my own needs more clearly and invite others into them. As Kevan expressed, this isn't just for help where I'm lacking, although it includes that. It's also about inviting others into my weaknesses in a way that God can use—both to deepen our friendship and to grow us together in the way of Christ. That vulnerability requires humility and courage beyond what's natural for me.

Second, I'm also asking for God's help to see and respond to others' needs more fully too. The spotlight of my thought life is so often fixed on my own list of to-dos and present concerns and petty interests. I

---

4. 1 John 4:19.

easily miss the needs right under my nose, even of those nearest to me, let alone others in my church or community who are struggling onward with brave smiles. I need greater attentiveness and discernment than I possess to notice those needs. I also need His grace to respond gladly, especially when doing so displaces my priorities and schedule.

At best, these prayers start my day but are also interwoven throughout it. As I pull up to a coffee shop to meet a friend or swipe to answer a phone call, I can descend for a moment into the recesses of my heart. *Lord, please bless Steve. Show me what he needs most and how I can help. Please bring good to him through me and also to me through him.*

Along with these prayers—more accurately, as *part* of these prayers—I know I must also listen. That can include pausing in attentive silence. But it also includes applying my own thinking with creativity while asking the Holy Spirit to guide me. Verses like "Let us consider how we may spur one another on to love and good deeds"[5] and many others carry a strong current of intentionality, planning, and deliberate action. Taking time to listen and jot down plans with a journal or notepad can be a great help.

Finally, once we've sensed God pointing toward an action, however small, we must give no place for delay. We'll harm ourselves if we do. We don't need to see the whole trail to take a step. You may already have a sense of what that step may be. Perhaps it's asking a friend to pray for a struggle you've never shared before or requesting their help with a simple task. Maybe you've also noticed a way you can step into their needs—a timely gift or encouraging word or spending a morning to help them with a task you know they've dreaded.

Our final aim is not merely to do a smattering of serendipitous acts here and there. It is to grow more like Jesus day by day. We want to become the kind of person who, like Him, lives fully within the dance

---

5. Heb. 10:24 NIV.

of giving and receiving, vulnerability and service, needs expressed and needs met, bearing each other's burdens . . . and in all this feeling our hearts grow more joyfully intimate with one another and our Maker. The music is playing. Let's take to the dance floor!

Jedd Medefind
President, Christian Alliance for Orphans

# Discussion Questions

1. What images, words, memories, or feelings come to mind for you when you hear the word *need*? How are these different from what they were before reading this book?

2. What is the hardest part for you about receiving care or having your needs met by someone else? What are your motivations and/or hesitations when it comes to meeting the needs of others?

3. What stands out to you most about the ministry Jesus had through His hospitality of need? How does this impact your understanding of Jesus' love for you and others?

4. How does biblical hospitality contrast with hospitality as it is understood in your community or culture? In what ways has this book encouraged you to invite others into your own life?

# Share Your Testimony with Us

We would love to hear from you! After reading this book, please take some time to consider how you have experienced the hospitality of need in your own life and community. Then, share with us online. Scan the QR code below or go to thehospitalityofneed.com and submit your testimony!

# Acknowledgments

This book has been several years in the making, has taken many forms along the way, and has been carried through by various people we'd like to thank. Right out of the gate, thank you to our families (the Chandlers, Sheltons, McGunnigals, and Milanos) for your tireless love and support, especially our parents and Tommy's amazing kids.

Then, to our friends, some of you were named in this book, and some were not, but all of you are priceless contributors to who we are. A special thanks to Scott Hasenbalg, Douglas McKelvey, and Jedd Medefind for working out these ideas with Kevan early on.

To Catherine Parks and the folks at Moody Publishers for taking a chance on us. The We Carry Kevan board, crew, and audience for believing these stories needed to be told. The Rabbit Room, Nashville Friends of L'Abri, and Live Oaks Bible Church for giving us platforms to share our initial drafts in lectures, sessions, and sermons. To Stephen P. Brown, the Dorris family, and both Bristow families for affording us opportunities to hide away and write.

A huge thank you to our wives, Katie and Mara, who have cheered us on with patience and grace. We would be nothing without you by our sides.

And our eternal thanks to Jesus Christ: our sweet Savior, Wonderful Counselor, and Mighty King.

# WE CARRY KEVAN

In the summer of 2016, Kevan Chandler and his friends took a trip across Europe, the adventures of which are shared briefly here and there in this book. They left his wheelchair at home, and his friends carried him for three weeks in a backpack. "We Carry Kevan" was the name of their campaign to raise funds and awareness for the trip. The idea took off, catching worldwide media attention. Kevan and his friends began hearing from families all over the world, asking two questions...

*1. Where did you get this backpack?*

*2. Where did you get these friends?*

To answer these two questions,
**We Carry Kevan** was established as a 501c3 nonprofit organization in 2017. The mission: to mobilize individuals with disabilities by redefining accessibility to be a cooperative effort. **People helping people.**

Learn more of this incredible story and see how you can join the adventure at

*WeCarryKevan.org*

# You finished reading!

Did this book help you in some way? If so, please consider writing an honest review wherever you purchase your books. Your review gets this book into the hands of more readers and helps us continue to create biblically faithful resources.

## Moody Publishers books help fund the training of students for ministry around the world.

The **Moody Bible Institute** is one of the most well-known Christian institutions in the world, training thousands of young people to faithfully serve Christ wherever He calls them. And when you buy and read a book from Moody Publishers, you're helping make that vital ministry training possible.

### Continue to dive into the Word, *anytime, anywhere.*

Find what you need to take your next step in your walk with Christ: from uplifting music to sound preaching, our programs are designed to help you right when you need it.

Download the **Moody Radio App** and start listening today!

 MOODY Publishers    MOODY Bible Institute    MOODY Radio